Diamonds in a Dunghill
The Simple Truths

Tony Hassall

Order this book online at www.trafford.com
or email orders@trafford.com

Most Trafford titles are also available at major online book retailers.

Printed in the United States of America.

ISBN: 978-1-4669-7282-7 (sc)
ISBN: 978-1-4669-7281-0 (e)

Trafford rev. 12/19/2012

 www.trafford.com

North America & international
toll-free: 1 888 232 4444 (USA & Canada)
phone: 250 383 6864 ♦ fax: 812 355 4082

Contents

Dedication

This book is dedicated to my beloved wife Julia, to my son Michael and his wife Leigh, to my two beautiful granddaughters Paige and Blair and to Nikki who, though no longer with us, has remained my greatest inspiration.

Acknowledgements

Above all I owe heartfelt thanks to my lovely wife Julia who has for more than thirty-five years been my best friend and confidant. I also acknowledge other members of my family who have helped to make me what I am. In particular I acknowledge my son Michael who has been a source of great strength to me. Thank you to the authors of the many wonderful books I have read who have kept the teachings of the great ones alive. Thank you also to my friends and acquaintances who have contributed to my human experience and who have inspired my stories. Thank you also to Penny for her work in editing and proof reading this book.

Foreword

In this book people are generally referred to in the male gender. This is to be read in the context of 'mankind' and not taken as implying male superiority. This is done for ease of reading and women should not take offence. The majority of this work applies to women equally as it does to men. However, as a man, I have a male perspective on life and this is naturally portrayed in my writing.

Introduction

Religion, more than anything else, divides mankind. Our intolerance, our hatred and our wars are often fuelled by religion. On the other hand religion has inspired our greatest men and women, our most noble deeds and our highest achievements. Can we remove the negative influences of religion from our world while still retaining the love, the meaning and the values that religion brings to our lives?

Most of the problems stem from a perception that our own religion is right and everyone else's religion is wrong. "My religion is true and yours is false." The claim may have some validity because, in absolute terms, there is only one "truth". The sun does come up in the morning, the planets revolve around the sun, and the Earth is not flat. These are facts with which we are all comfortable. They are facts that can be proven to most people's satisfaction.

The difficulty with religious ideas is that they usually concern concepts that are not easily proven. They are beliefs that may be true or false. We go to heaven/hell when we die or we don't, we are reincarnated or we are not, Christ was a God or He wasn't, Muhammad was a true prophet of God or he wasn't, the Pope has the authority of God or he doesn't. These are examples of theological concepts that separate religions. None can be proven definitively yet the proponents of each religion hold fast to their beliefs about them as absolute truths. But who is right? We can't all be right.

The reality is that there are truths and falsehoods in all religions and although some religions contain more truth than others, none is totally right and none is totally wrong. However, under close examination we find that most of the contradictions concern theological dogma. Yet, hidden among the clouds of dogma, runs a common thread of truth.

This book attempts to cut through the layers of dogma to get to the underlying truths that really matter. Looking for the truth is like panning for gold. When we carefully sluice out the rocks and sands we see the shining precious nuggets of truth.

Real truths are mostly about doing what's right. Most people have good intentions and want to do what they believe is right. All religious authorities teach us their version of what's right. But what is right? Is it going to church on Sunday? Is it fighting for our country? Is it being faithful to our spouse? In the end it's up to each of us to decide. But we must examine the evidence using our powers of reason and our experiences to help us, not the dogmas of any religious authority. I trust this book will help you to decide for yourself dear reader, to use sound judgement in making your everyday decisions, in the light of the teachings of some of our great sages of the past who have considered these questions and whose insights appear in this book.

Faith, or rather lack of it, is a dilemma facing our modern world. Many of our problems including depression, despair and even criminal behaviour can be attributed to a lack of faith. Many thinking people have rejected faith because of the dogma that is associated with religion and they have thrown the baby out with the bath water. But we can, if we so desire, go back to the basics, to the raw and simple truths taught to us and demonstrated by the founders of the world's great religions. Life's great truths are really quite simple and are available to us all if we will only look.

There is also, in our modern age, a revival of religious fundamentalism, which is perhaps a greater problem than lack of faith because it breeds intolerance and hatred. In the middle ages it drove the murderous inquisition of the Church and today it drives Islamic extremism, which threatens our civilisation, our freedom and our very existence.

Religious extremism that manifests in hatred and intolerance is like a dreadful disease. Sadly it is very difficult to treat. The root of the problem is that fundamentalists are indoctrinated with ideas very early in their lives making reasoning with them almost impossible. This is easy to prove, you just need to listen to the children of extremists. They are expressing the same hatred as their elders, even before they are old enough to understand the issues.

This highlights a special problem. We must educate not just ourselves, but more importantly our children, for they are our future.

Our children need to develop a strong faith and good values, without being indoctrinated with religious dogma that leads to intolerance and hatred.

In this book Bill continues his search for wisdom from where he left off in "A Freethinkers Search for Wisdom and Truth" and "The Science Junto." In this case he seeks the "natural religion" or truth that is contained within most religions of the world, hidden under piles of theological dogma. Bill searches for the meaning of life and divines some simple truths that the great teachers have been trying to teach us over and over again.

Chapter 1—Revelations

"People only see what they are prepared to see" Ralph Waldo Emerson

Bill deftly cast his line upstream into the riffle in the stream, his dry fly landing delicately in the exact spot he intended, just beyond where he had seen the mouth of a trout rise to take a floating insect. He was fishing in the picturesque Guy Fawkes River, a wilderness area in the Northern Rivers region of New South Wales. The fishing here wasn't as exciting as the fast flowing New Zealand rivers he had fished in his youth, but it was nonetheless satisfying and the surroundings were utterly serene. More importantly it was reasonably accessible to him, being only a few hours drive from where he lived in Southern Queensland.

While the fish here were relatively small, it required great skill to catch them. The gently flowing water meant that very light tackle was required so that a fly could be presented to an unsuspecting trout without alarming it. He watched carefully as the tiny lure floated back towards him, sighing contentedly, taking in the beauty and tranquillity of his surroundings. He wondered how this tiny stream could have carved out such a massive deep gorge, the banks of which climbed steeply up to the tableland five hundred metres above.

At the next cast his heart leapt at the thrilling yet familiar sight of a ripple in the surface that engulfed his fly. He waited momentarily and then gently flicked his carbon fibre rod to set the hook firmly in the mouth of the unfortunate trout.

He shouted excitedly to attract the attention of his friend Aaron who was fishing the next pool upstream. Aaron, who was yet to catch anything, called back "You lucky bugger, you're onto one!" He reeled in his own line and came over to watch as Bill skilfully played the fish, letting it run when necessary so as not to break the light line, but at the same time holding it back somewhat to stop it racing into a snag.

Bill beamed as he finally flicked the flapping fish onto the bank. It was about three pounds, which was quite a big fish in these parts. "I think I'll clean it right away and we'll have it for dinner" Bill declared as Aaron looked on, perhaps a little enviously. They had been fishing most of the day and as it was now dusk there was little chance of him catching one.

Bill waded out into a shallow backwater to clean the fish and immediately regretted that he had taken off his boots as his bare feet started to sink into a muddy patch. Suddenly his heart stopped. A chilling sensation shot up his spine as he felt a strong slithering movement under his bare foot. "Holy crap!" he shouted, as the writhing body of a black snake wound itself around his legs. His adrenalin-enhanced leap from the water approached the speed of light. When he was safely on the bank Bill turned to see the snake's long tail still thrashing about in the water. Bill turned to Aaron who was roaring with laughter.

"It's not funny!" Bill complained indignantly. "What if it had bitten me? I'd have a job getting to a hospital from here. Remember that time you almost died from a snake bite?"

"Sorry Bill" Aaron chuckled; now regaining his composure. "It was the look on your face as you jumped out of the water. What a classic. Actually that one probably wouldn't have killed you. The red bellies are venomous but rarely deadly. You must have pushed its head into the mud I reckon. That's why it didn't bite you. The poor thing had trouble freeing itself."

They turned to watch as the snake, now clearly visible, appeared to extract itself from the mud and slither quietly away. "I'll never get used to snakes" Bill shuddered.

"Lucky you flung that fish onto the bank rather than into the water in your panic" Aaron remarked as he picked up the fish and handed it to Bill.

Darkness was creeping up quickly as they made their way back to the camp site, which thankfully was quite close, and Bill was glad to see their tent come into view. After a delicious trout dinner they retired early, looking forward to an early start in the morning.

Bill awoke in pitch blackness to the almost deafening sound of torrential rain. Aaron was already up, hurriedly breaking camp. "Better pack up!" he shouted "we need to move to higher ground.

If a flash flood comes down this river we're going to get washed away."

Bill shouted his agreement, located his torch, frantically threw his gear into his pack and helped Aaron take down the tent. They scrambled through the bush away from the stream, which was now roaring. Both sides to the gorge were quite steep but the two men stumbled on a game trail that took them up away from the valley floor and found themselves on a small plateau that seemed to be an adequate height above river level.

"This looks OK" Bill yelled as they did their best to pitch the tent. They spent the rest of the night wet and uncomfortable on the uneven rocky ground. Constant dripping from the tent made any further sleep impossible.

When dawn broke the rain had finally stopped, but the little mountain stream was now a raging torrent. "Looks like we're going to have to sit this out for a while" Bill said.

"Reckon you're right" Aaron agreed. "At least now the rain's stopped we can dry out and make ourselves a bit more comfortable."

"Looks like we won't be doing any more fishing" Bill sighed.

"Oh well, there's always next time" Aaron grinned. "It's been fun anyway."

Bill smiled; he loved the way Aaron was always so positive. This was only one of the qualities Bill liked about him. He had become a close friend and to some extent a mentor to Bill over the last few years. He was a little older than Bill, in his late fifties but with the fitness and energy of a much younger man.

"Just as well we brought this bottle of Scotch" Aaron interrupted Bill's thoughts as he poured a generous slug into Bill's coffee. They had managed to get a fire going and though meagre owing to the wetness of the wood, it gave them comfort. As was often the case their conversation turned to spiritual matters.

Bill had often wondered about the source of Aaron's religious beliefs and took the opportunity to quiz him. "You said once that you took some of your spiritual ideas from a small Christian sect in the USA. Are you willing to tell me which one it is?"

Aaron was normally quite cagey about the source of his beliefs but the whiskey was taking its toll. "Yes, well if you must know, I read a book many years ago called "The Ultimate Frontier" and it had a major effect on me."

"So that's it!" Bill replied, as if Aaron had made a great revelation, and then with a little more circumspection continued "Of course I've read that book too and we discussed it in my old email group. But didn't the author Eklal Kueshana, alias Richard Kieninger, get discredited for making some major prophesies that never came true?"

Aaron scratched his chin and stared into the fire looking like he didn't really want to get into this conversation. "Sure" he finally replied, "but that doesn't necessarily negate the truth of the teaching. Richard Kieninger has been discredited in many ways. In fact, we now know that he plagiarised most of the material for his book from the Lemurian Fellowship."

"I'm aware of that" Bill responded "and didn't he get into trouble with his own community for womanising and so on?"

"Sure, and for all we know his story was a pack of lies, the way he wove himself into the Lemurian Philosophy making himself out to be some kind of "chosen one." It really was a gross deception to all his followers and readers. Yet, at the same time, he was the one that put these profound ideas out in the public domain. If he hadn't done that the philosophy would only be available to the tiny number of people who enrol in the Lemurian Fellowship's courses. Also the fact that he was a student of theirs for many years indicates to me that he at least started out as a genuine seeker of truth and he seems to have spent most of his life in an effort to uplift mankind."

"Maybe he became corrupted along the way" Bill suggested. "Perhaps he originally intended "The Ultimate Frontier" to be a work of fiction, a kind of allegory or parable to illustrate the ideas he had learned from the Lemurian Fellowship. But then he found, to get any attention, he needed to make out it was all true. And then he became so caught up in it all and had gained such a following that he felt he couldn't back out and tell the truth."

"That's possible" Aaron nodded, "but regardless of whether the story is true or not, to me what's important is the teaching and what appealed to me most was Kieninger's clarity, the way he explained the ideas. When you boil it down to the essence of the philosophy itself it's hard to fault.

There are some key concepts that I think make perfect sense, like the idea that the goal of human existence is the perfection of our souls and that the circumstances we find ourselves in and the challenges we face are those we need to conquer in order to advance."

"But we don't have to conquer it all first time around" Bill interrupted enthusiastically "because the concepts of reincarnation and karma mean that we have many lifetimes to perfect our souls."

"Absolutely, but if we dodge our problems they will keep coming back to us until we do conquer them. The other notions I like are that morality is a logical universal code that can be derived by all wise men, rather than being a blind compliance to some dogma and that salvation comes from right thoughts and actions rather than from some belief, ritual or obeisance to a particular church."

"Makes sense to me," Bill agreed "I also like the idea that our circumstances and everything we enjoy or suffer stems from our own individual thoughts and actions."

"Sure" Aaron added, "and when those thoughts and actions stem from love and faith then we can achieve almost anything. But there's also the overriding concept of self-discipline, that none of this can work without self-discipline."

"Yeah, maybe that's what Kieninger lacked" Bill agreed. "Where do you think these ideas originated in the first place though? I mean did he plagiarise it all from the Lemurian Fellowship or was some of it from other religions or really from the Brotherhoods. Do the Brotherhoods even exist? Is there really a group of advanced Saints or Masters watching over us trying to encourage and uplift mankind?"

"There are quite a few unanswered questions" Aaron replied "but I do believe the Brotherhoods exist. Whether they had anything to do with Kieninger, I can't say. When you think about it, his claim about the source of the ideas is not unlike the origins of much religious thought. A lot of it is said to be "revealed" from God or some other higher source. Many religions and schisms have been founded like this, for example Mormonism, Islam and even some of the Bible such as St John's Revelation and so on."

Bill nodded "Sure but how can we tell what's true and what's false or even if any of it's true?"

Aaron stared thoughtfully into the fire "Obviously we can't know for sure about any "revealed truth." We can only keep testing the ideas against our observations using the power of reason and experience. Kieninger himself always stressed that we should do this."

They sat silently for some time before Bill finally suggested "Maybe Kieninger was just a pawn in all this and his intentions are irrelevant. Perhaps the ideas just needed to make the light of day and Kieninger was the instrument."

"You could be right Bill. God works in mysterious ways, as they say."

Bill got up to throw more wood on the fire. "OK then, if we accept that Kieninger pinched most of the ideas from the Lemurian Fellowship, where did they get them? How much do you know about them?"

"Actually not very much" Aaron replied. "To tell you the truth I once applied to take their course of study, but they turned me down. Apparently they don't accept anyone that mentions they've had any association with Richard Kieninger or his book."

"It would be interesting to find out more about them" Bill suggested.

There was no response from Aaron. Bill looked over to see he had drifted off to sleep and was snoring peacefully.

"Whiskey must have got to him" he chuckled to himself.

Bill spent much of the rest of the day in reflection and making notes on their discussions. When Aaron woke some hours later they shifted their camp to a more comfortable position nearer the river which had already started to go down. They cooked a hearty feast from their remaining provisions and slept comfortably through the night.

The next morning the river looked negotiable enough for their long walk back to civilisation. After a strenuous trek along the gorge they scrambled up the steep and, in places, treacherous cliff to where the Guy Fawkes River plunged hundreds of metres over the escarpment in a beautiful three-tiered waterfall known as Ebor Falls. When they finally reached the top, they looked back to admire the breathtaking view. There was still a substantial flow of water cascading down into the depths of the valley.

"Spectacular isn't it" Aaron said.

"Magnificent" Bill agreed. "I'd like to just spend a little time alone here to reflect if you don't mind, this place has a special meaning to me."

"Sure no problem" Aaron replied, "I'll go and pack the car."

Bill gazed back out over the gorge, which zigzagged off into the distance. It was forest as far as the eye could see, over which seemed to hang a permanent blue-green haze. In the other direction the sun glinted on the smooth water that was the upper reaches of the river above the falls; a peaceful grassy stream that meandered lazily over the tablelands.

As he continued to stare out across the stunning scene he slipped into a daydream. He drifted back in his memory, to another time, to the first time he had been in this magical place. It was almost a decade ago, but he recalled it so vividly it could have been yesterday. The weather had been different that day. It was cold and misty with a light drizzle. He remembered looking for the falls but he couldn't see them owing to the mist. He had been walking by this very spot where he now sat in contemplation.

It had been odd; it was a feeling as if he had wandered through into another world, a surreal alternative reality. He could still hear the voices of his teenage daughter Natalie and her friend Patricia as they laughed and chatted nearby. Their voices seemed far away and yet at the same time an integral part of the scene and above all familiar. Everything was familiar. The experience was like an extended déjà vu. He had occasionally experienced such a mystical event before but never this vividly. He mused that perhaps there were some places in the world that had a kind of unexplainable mystical quality and this was one of them. He remembered how the shroud of mist had cleared to reveal the bridal veil of the top two tiers of the falls. He seemed to snap back to reality as Natalie had caught up to him and said "Beautiful isn't it Dad."

Bill knew he would never again experience such a magical moment with his daughter, at least in this life, because a few months later Natalie had been killed in a tragic car accident. Bill felt the anguish and pain at his loss of her come flooding back to him. He longed to talk to her, but instead said a little prayer in her memory. He imagined he could still hear Natalie and her friend giggling in the mist behind him. But that was another time and time cannot go backwards. Natalie had moved on and was now surely either waiting in another dimension or perhaps her soul had already come back as a baby girl somewhere. Such were Bill's beliefs that kept him sane and, for the most part, a happy man. He was particularly happy to have had this lovely daughter in his life for twenty years.

He awoke from his daydream to the sound of Aaron's voice saying "are you right to go mate?" He was obviously keen to get going; they were running late and he probably had lots to do because he was getting married in a few days.

Aaron's wedding took place as planned the following weekend. It was an intimate affair in a small chapel in a country town near where Aaron ran an outdoor adventure camp for young people. Bill felt rather pleased with himself as he watched the couple take their vows. It was he who had introduced them and it seemed they were just made for each other.

As they exited the chapel Bill couldn't help noticing a stunning looking young woman who had come in late and was now smiling radiantly at Bill. He felt a wave of passionate emotion sweep over him as he recognised Angela, a woman who some years before had been a member of Bill's email group, the same group where he had met Aaron.

As they mingled outside Angela came up to Bill who had manoeuvred himself clear of the crowd. "So how are you, handsome?" she beamed as she gave him a peck on the cheek.

"I'm fine" Bill stammered "It's lovely to see you Angela. You haven't changed a bit. You still have that perfect figure and that gorgeous pretty face. How do you do it?"

"Thanks, quite a lot of exercise actually" she laughed. "It's lovely to see you too. It's been a long time."

"Too long" Bill nodded just as they were interrupted. The opportunity to talk further with Angela was gone for the time being but Bill whispered to her that he would try to catch up with her later.

As they left for the reception Sarah, Bill's wife, asked him who was the woman he had been talking to.

"Oh that was Angela" Bill replied. "You remember she used to be in my email group."

"Is she the one you met up with in Sydney that time?" Sarah asked curiously.

"Yes" Bill responded hesitantly "that time I met with Aaron, Ravi and Angela."

This was true but Bill found himself fighting pangs of guilt from what he had left unsaid. There had been another occasion on which he had met with Angela in Sydney, just the two of them. They had had dinner together, and although nothing further had eventuated, it was an evening that stood out in Bill's memory.

"She seems to like you" Sarah said softly.

"I . . . I guess so" Bill stuttered.

Sarah smiled at Bill's obvious embarrassment.

"I love you darling" Bill whispered. "You're the love of my life."

"I know" Sarah smiled.

At the reception Bill and Sarah found themselves seated next to Hamish. Bill doubted this was a coincidence because Hamish seemed to have a way of mysteriously showing up whenever Bill was troubled about something. On this occasion there were some important questions that Bill wanted to put to Hamish.

Hamish was quite elderly with silvery white hair and his face had the pronounced creases of character gained from a full life, yet at the same time, having a kind of youthful exuberant glow. Bill knew him as the leader of the Junto, a secret organisation dedicated to the betterment of mankind. Bill was now himself a member of the Junto and it had become an overarching influence in his life. Hamish as its leader was held by Bill in the very highest regard. He had become like a father figure, a wise confidant with whom Bill felt he could discuss anything.

At last the formalities of the wedding were over, the guests were either dancing or engaged in social discourse and Sarah was chatting to friends. Bill was finally able to ask Hamish the questions that had been burning on his mind.

"Hamish, when I was fishing with Aaron, he told me about the source of some of his religious beliefs."

"Oh, and what was that?"

"Well a lot of it seems to have come from the book "The Ultimate Frontier.""

"Uh huh" Hamish replied as if saying "so what."

"Well I was a bit surprised you know, I thought he must have got his beliefs from some profound source, or maybe even from you."

"What made you think that?" Hamish asked, expressing surprise.

"I guess it's because of the Junto and because he seems to have similar ideas to you."

"Yes I'm sure that Aaron and I do have much in common in our views, but I don't think our beliefs are identical. The Junto doesn't require that we have the same religious beliefs, as you know. Of course we all believe the tenets of our creed including that we believe in God and so on, but beyond that we are free to believe whatever we like.

As Truth seekers, we will naturally reach the same conclusions in the end about the nature of existence, on our journey towards the absolute Truth. We have many beliefs in common but not everything is the same. We may not even hold the same views about right and wrong. As you know the Junto is an open forum where we can debate right and wrong courses of action. This is as it should be. No one religion, group or philosophy has the absolute Truth."

Bill interrupted "but some groups are closer to the Truth than others."

19

"Certainly, but this is not a static thing. Groups change over time. A religious organisation may start out based on truth, right thinking and goodness but it may not always stay that way. Misguided and sometimes evil people can and do take over good groups and lead them down the wrong path. So a good group can become bad with bad leadership. Also sometimes the leaders of groups who start off with good intentions become corrupted by greed and power. History is littered with examples, spanning almost every nation and religion."

"Like the Spanish Inquisition and so on" Bill suggested.

"Exactly!"

"Getting back to Aaron's beliefs and their source, could this be an example of what we're talking about?"

"What do you think of Aaron's faith and beliefs?" Hamish asked, evading the question.

"Well I think many of the ideas are great, but having come from a dubious source, how close can they be to the Truth? I mean the way the leader of that cult became discredited for lying and so on."

"What do you mean by dubious?" Hamish enquired.

"I mean Kieninger, his lies and that he said he got it from the Brotherhoods. But the source turned out to be the Lemurian Fellowship, which seems to have dubious origins itself. They claim their book "The Sun Rises" is the truth gleaned from the Akashic record by its author Robert Stelle."

"And you think this is unlikely?" Hamish asked.

"Yeah, I think there's some pretty farfetched stuff in that book. It's a good story though and has some sound moral guidance."

"Do you think there's farfetched information in other philosophies?" Hamish asked.

"Sure, I suppose so. Do you mean we need to figure out what's true and what's false from all religions and philosophies?"

"Yes."

"That's what Aaron says."

"I agree with Aaron" Hamish replied. "There are countless religions and philosophies in the world and, while each contains some truth, none is in possession of all the Truth. In the end does it really matter about the source of the truth? Surely it is the Truth itself that matters."

"I guess so. But at the same time I'd love to know if there really are noble sources such as the Brotherhoods proclaimed by Kieninger and the Lemurian Fellowship."

"I believe there are" Hamish smiled.

"Do the Brotherhoods have anything to do with the Junto?" Bill had been dying to ask this question.

Hamish again evaded the question. "Bill, there are many groups working towards the betterment of mankind, including the Junto. The Junto is the Junto and you are aware of its objectives."

Bill wasn't at all satisfied with Hamish's answer and pursued his line of questioning. "Yes but are we linked to other groups?"

"I can't give you an answer to that question right now. It's not as simple as you might think."

Hamish said these words with an air of finality that indicated to Bill that this discussion was now closed.

They were silent for a time and the background noise of the wedding reception, which had previously seemed remote, now encroached on them.

"There's something else I wanted to ask you about Hamish."

"Fire away, but don't be disappointed if I don't know the answer. I don't know everything" Hamish chuckled.

"It's about the Great Pyramid of Giza and its purpose."

"There are a lot of theories about the Great Pyramid" Hamish commented.

"Aaron thinks it has a prophetic purpose" Bill replied.

"What do you think?"

"I'm not so sure" Bill responded. "I'm sceptical about any kind of prophesy these days. I have my own theory about the purpose of the Great Pyramid." He explained his theory to Hamish that related to the meaning of human life.

"It sounds like a good theory. You have put a lot of research and thought into it."

"But is it true?" Bill asked emphatically.

"What makes you think I know the answer to that?" Hamish looked bemused.

"Aaron thought you might know" Bill stammered.

"Like I said I don't have all the answers" Hamish laughed. "You're asking me if the Great Pyramid is a beacon for the meaning of human life. That's a pretty big question. First of all you need to figure out the meaning of life! Have you figured this out for yourself?"

Bill started to feel a little silly. "I don't know, maybe, I'm still searching I guess."

"Continue your search and if you are earnestly looking for the Truth you will find it" Hamish said kindly.

Bill felt a little frustrated. He had expected a more definitive answer from Hamish. He stared into his empty glass. He had by now drunk more wine than he should have and started to get a little emotional.

"Hamish I have been searching! And I've also been doing my best for the Science Junto. But to tell you the truth I get disillusioned at times. I sometimes feel that I'm beating my head against a brick wall. No one wants to listen to me or read my books."

"Don't be disheartened Bill. It might seem like we're losing the battle, but that's no reason to give up. In fact there's more reason than ever for you to stick to your guns and to speak out. The loud voices of unreason coming from the atheists on the one side and the religious extremists on the other require our full attention. There are huge stakes here: the future of mankind, the souls of humanity.

Don't worry too much about who reads your books. If they are available, the right people will eventually come across them, I assure you. There may be only a small number of people who will read your books and take on the ideas, but these are important people. They are people who are ready for these ideas, who are at a certain level in their development as human beings. You can't help everyone. The masses of humanity are not ready to take on these ideas. Leave the masses to others who are better suited to the task."

"So you think I should continue my fight."

"Absolutely, in fact we need you now more than ever. What about your studies in science, how's that going?"

"I'm feeling frustrated with that too. I used to be passionate about science but I'm not sure if this is what I should be doing right now. My mind keeps coming back to spiritual matters and science just seems to be a distraction. What should I do?"

"What do you want to do?"

"I've been thinking about writing a book about faith, but I don't know if I can do it and I don't know where to start" Bill complained.

"That sounds like a good idea" Hamish replied. "Faith is certainly in crisis. On the one hand there's a general lack of faith contributing to despair and the breakdown of society and moral values. On the other hand we have religious extremism leading to hatred and intolerance. Perhaps the right kind of book would make a difference. Why don't you start right now? You can do it. Be confident, be strong, we are with you!" Hamish concluded warmly.

At this point Sarah returned to her seat and said "Sorry to interrupt your conversation gentlemen, but they're about to cut the cake."

After the brief ritual people started to move around the room and Bill took the opportunity to talk to Angela who had been sitting on the other side of the room. They had exchanged glances several times during the evening and now they were close together their eyes locked in a lingering mutual stare that neither of them seemed to want to relinquish.

"Windows to the soul" Bill muttered the cliché out loud without even thinking.

"Sorry, what?" Angela asked cheekily.

"Oh nothing" he replied meekly as he finally blinked and tore his eyes away. He didn't know why he had such a strong attraction to Angela. The mystery was beyond him. One thing he knew for sure was that it hadn't faded with time. He had an almost overwhelming desire to kiss her, but he knew he couldn't possibly act on it.

"Are you happy Bill?" she asked finally.

"Yes I'm fine" Bill gulped. "Sarah and I are fine" he added as if to remind her he was married.

She nodded "that's good, I'm glad you're happy. I haven't been very happy myself but I'm hoping things will improve. I'm going away to Egypt. I have a one-year contract working for a travel company."

"Oh you'll have to send me your address" Bill said genuinely "you never know when I might get back there myself. I have some unfinished business . . . ."

Angela interrupted "Oh please do come and see me in Egypt" she said as she reached out and squeezed his hand. His heart pounded as he looked once more into her glistening eyes.

Bill was brought back to reality by another hand being placed firmly on his elbow. "Oh hi Sarah" he mumbled "this is Angela."

Chapter 2—The Lemurian

"To love our neighbor as ourselves is such a truth for regulating human society, that by that alone one might determine all the cases in social morality" John Locke

After the wedding Bill found it increasingly difficult to focus on his scientific research. Hamish's words kept churning over in his mind "Start right now, you can do it."

That's all very well for him to say Bill pondered, but where do I start?

"Penny for your thoughts Bill" Sarah said as she brought him his morning coffee. She could see that he was ruminating about something.

"I want to write a book about faith that could help others, but there are so many books already. Who am I to think mine could be different?"

Sarah smiled encouragingly "I think your strength is in your worldly experiences. You've led an interesting life, seen many places, and suffered lots of heartache. You haven't been sheltered in any particular sect. Your books are worthy because they come from your heart, from your life's experience."

"Thanks" Bill grinned gratefully "I needed that. But my experience with people of faith has been limited."

"That's never stopped you before" Sarah chirped. "Maybe we could do some more travel and meet some."

Bill chuckled "Is that a hint?" He knew Sarah enjoyed travel and especially loved to accompany him on his adventures. "You might be onto something there. I could start by investigating Aaron's religion and its various schisms. He's been a big influence on me and I'd like to see where it all came from. There are a lot of questions that even Aaron doesn't know the answers to. It all started in America and we've never really travelled in the USA."

"Sounds exciting" Sarah responded "like a quest for the truth."

"Yeah a quest . . ." Bill mused; his thoughts drifting back again to Hamish's words: A quest for the truth, but also a quest for the meaning of life. "Perhaps this could be the start of a wider search" he said out loud.

"You mean for your book?" Sarah asked.

"Yes, but I mean a search for the meaning of life."

"The meaning of life!" Sarah exclaimed. "Whew that's a big question, how do you propose to find that?"

"Err . . ." Bill stammered "I have this idea that if I ask the right people I will find it. I believe that Aaron's religion claims to know the meaning of life. So perhaps that's a good place to start. I'll ask them and then put the same question to followers of other religions. What do you reckon?"

Sarah looked sceptical but readily agreed that the best thing to do was to go on a trip to the USA as soon as possible.

Bill was able to postpone his research and within a few weeks they had landed in Los Angeles and were on their way to Ramona California, the home of the Lemurian Fellowship. In a few hours, guided by the GPS they found themselves at the entrance to the Lemurian Fellowship.

"Should we go in?" Bill hesitated. He had asked Aaron about it and was advised that the Fellowship did not welcome visitors. Some friends of his had actually been chased off the property at one stage.

"We've come all this way, of course we're going in" Sarah insisted.

Bill turned into the neatly maintained entranceway rather apprehensively. They drove up the steep driveway to a group of buildings that was hidden from the road. The property was obviously well cared for, with large paved areas interrupted by bordered gardens with beautiful shrubs and trees. The setting was tranquil and secluded, overlooking bushy hills with rocky outcrops, somewhat reminiscent of Bill and Sarah's own property in Australia.

They arrived at a parking area with a sign pointing to an office. "That looks promising" Sarah suggested. "If they have an office they must have visitors. Can you see anyone around?"

Bill was still feeling anxious. Aaron had warned him that they were very sensitive about anyone who had come into contact with the "Richard Kieninger sect."

"Can I help you?" a voice called out, startling Bill as he turned to see a man walking quite hurriedly up the path towards them. Bill replied "Yes, hello we've heard about your organisation and are interested to learn more."

The man, who appeared to be in his sixties though fit looking, stared at Bill and Sarah quite suspiciously for a few seconds, his eyes piercing, as if trying to read their minds. Then he smiled and introduced himself as Raymond. He spoke in a kindly and friendly manner but at the same time seemed guarded and perhaps slightly nervous. He asked where they were from and seemed genuinely interested when Bill said they were from Australia.

"What do you already know about us?" Raymond enquired when Bill had introduced himself and Sarah.

"Well . . ." Bill replied hesitantly, his mind racing. How much should I say, he thought to himself. I don't want to lie but I don't want to reveal too much either or he might throw us out. "I've read "The Sun Rises," looked you up on the internet and have read some of your literature" he stammered. This was all true and he had read some introductory literature that Aaron had given him from when he had enquired about taking the course of study offered by the Lemurian Fellowship.

This seemed to satisfy Raymond and he appeared to relax more and asked them if they would like a coffee.

"Thank you" Sarah interjected, "That would be lovely, we've had a long drive."

Raymond did not invite them into the office but showed them an outdoor table and said he would bring the coffee out to them presently.

"He seems nice" Sarah whispered as they waited "And I thought I detected there was some kind of connection between you and him as you talked."

"Do you think so?" Bill responded. "I'm not so sure. I don't know where I stand with him. I'm certainly not going to say anything about our mission or the schisms and so on."

Sarah nodded as Raymond returned with three coffees. "So, where are you up to with your truth studies Bill?" he asked as he joined them at the table.

Bill was taken aback by Raymond's directness but replied honestly that he was very interested in the Lemurian philosophy and that it seemed more sensible than any other belief systems he had studied.

"Oh," Raymond smiled "What aspects appeal to you most?"

"Well for a start I like that you believe in reincarnation" Bill remarked.

"Of course" Raymond continued, "It's impossible to master this human existence in just one lifetime. The only way it can make sense is that we must get more than one life to achieve it."

"Makes sense to me" Bill agreed. "Are you implying that the meaning of life is for us to master this existence?"

"Yes, we believe we are here on this earth to master this physical plane of existence by learning all the lessons of this physical world. Once we have mastered this physical world we are ready for the next level of existence. It's all about advancing our spirit or soul through good works and learning by doing."

"Sounds logical" Bill agreed. "So is it about perfecting our souls?"

"Yes you could put it that way, but of course we have many lifetimes to achieve it."

"I had a friend once who was in a Christian sect that also believed in that goal, only he thought he had to do it in one lifetime" Bill commented.

Raymond chuckled "striving for perfection in one lifetime would put enormous pressure on a person."

"Yeah I think there were a lot of pressures in his sect."

"What do you mean?" Raymond enquired.

"Well I guess it's the cult thing" Bill responded, "where members are under the thumb of some control freak leader and pressured into cutting off contact with their family members who aren't in the cult. There's also a lot of fear involved. Members are terrified of being thrown out in the cold."

"Sadly those are common problems with exclusionist sects" Raymond agreed. "The effect on families can be profound. Of course we don't suffer such problems within the Lemurian Fellowship because members are free to come and go. We don't even ask that people give up their existing beliefs because they may be appropriate for where an individual currently is on their path and in their development as a human being. Above all we believe that interfering in the lives of others is against natural law."

"But doesn't that mean people could be clinging on to false beliefs?" Bill remarked.

"Yes of course, but in order to grow as human beings we need to figure out what the Truth really is for ourselves. If we had it handed to us on a plate we wouldn't really *know* it. We need to experience things to really know. The Lemurian Fellowship teaches a course of self study that provides students with a moral basis for living, but it is up to the individual to decide how to use these lessons in their lives. We don't actively recruit students unless they have approached us."

"How do people know you exist then?" Bill asked.

"We believe that those who are ready for our teaching will find us. Perhaps you are one of those people Bill. Have you thought about undertaking our course?"

Bill hesitated "I will give it some thought, maybe. But I'd like to ask you a little more about your philosophy. If our goal is to master this existence, how do we do that?"

"This is all covered in the course material, but essentially it's about building our character through practicing the twelve basic virtues and by learning and living in harmony with God's Universal Laws."

"I used to belong to a group that discussed such things" Bill interrupted. "We compared various lists of virtues in an effort to come up with a comprehensive list."

"Oh," Raymond expressed interest "and what did you come up with?"

"We ended up with a consensus of about twelve virtues too. The hard part was not so much figuring out what they were but putting them into practice."

Raymond laughed "yes that's the main problem for all of us. But do you feel you've achieved some success?"

Sarah, who had been quietly listening, interjected "yes he has . . . . a little" she added.

"Thanks Sarah" Bill grinned, "I know I have a long way to go. I think the best thing I got from the exercise was identifying the virtues I need to work on."

"Like humility" Sarah giggled.

"Yeah" Bill chuckled. "I tried to use Benjamin Franklin's methods towards self-improvement but lacked the self-discipline to persevere for long enough."

"It does require a diligent and concerted effort" Raymond agreed. "The Lemurian training places the utmost emphasis on the conscious development of the twelve virtues into one's character."

Bill nodded "I'm also interested in your views on the Universal Laws. I remember reading them in "The Sun Rises" and most of them seemed pretty sensible, but there are a couple that may be a little controversial."

"Which ones are those?" Raymond asked.

"First of all the law about non-interference causes conjecture."

Raymond nodded "The seventh law: *that no individual shall have the right to operate in the environment or personal affairs of another unless asked to do so by that person, and only where criminal or treasonable intent can be proved or the civil rights of another have been violated may the State or commonwealth as a whole operate or interfere in the personal affairs of an individual.* That is certainly the one that seems to cause the most heartache, not only for the ones who deliberately violate it like the power hungry cult leaders you mentioned, but also for well-intentioned do-gooders."

"Yes that's what I'm getting at. It's the "well-intentioned" interference that seems to be at the heart of the problem" Bill agreed.

"The road to Hell is paved with good intentions" Sarah murmured.

"Indeed, an interesting expression" Raymond acknowledged. "Of course we don't believe in Hell in the conventional sense, but this is the law most often broken by those who think they are doing the right thing."

Bill interrupted "But people often react as though this approach is heartless or unkind. If you see someone falling by the wayside and don't do anything to help, isn't it uncharitable and isn't charity a virtue?"

"That's true Bill and that's why learning to live by Gods Laws isn't easy. While they seem simple individually, real life situations can be complex and a decision may require a conflict between natural laws and, as you say, seem unvirtuous. Sometimes we have to choose "the lesser of two evils." Of course we should be charitable and kindly. But is it kindly to take away someone's free will by making decisions for them? Or is it charitable to help someone who is on the wrong path to continue down that wrong path?"

"Look I agree with you" Bill started but noticed that Sarah was shaking her head "I don't understand this law" she said. "Does that mean a mother can't protect her child?"

Raymond shook his head slowly "While they are children it may be OK, but once they are grown up it is exactly the same as interfering in any other adult's life. It is a difficult Law to get to grips with. The point is we need to be sparing in the help we give to others unless they ask for it. Sometimes it can appear mean to withhold your kindness but in the long run it may be the kindest thing to do for that person. The reason for the Law is that in this life, each person must uplift themselves. If we have it done for us we don't learn the lessons of life."

Sarah seemed unconvinced and sat back in her chair looking out at the scenery, appearing to distance herself somewhat from the remainder of the discussion as Bill continued "These laws that are given by Dr Stelle in "The Sun Rises," how do you know they are the right ones?"

"Fair point" Raymond conceded. "We believe that these Laws were given to Dr Stelle along with other Truths by the Brotherhoods."

"The Brotherhoods" Bill interrupted, "who are they?"

"The Brotherhoods are those advanced Masters or Saints who have gone before us and have already achieved the pinnacle of human development. Dr Robert Stelle was our contact with the Brotherhoods. But that's about all I can tell you right now."

Raymond paused, obviously not wanting to be questioned on the subject of the Brotherhoods, and continued "Getting back to Universal Laws, a key point is that they are discovered by man rather than made by man. They are similar to the physical laws of nature such as those discovered by Isaac Newton. We can never really prove one hundred percent that a law is absolute, but we can test the laws in our lives and observe outcomes in our own lives and in the lives of others around us. What other Universal Laws do you have a problem with?"

"There's the law about common ownership of natural resources" Bill replied. "It sounds a bit like communism to me."

"Ah yes the third law: *that all natural resources shall remain the property of the state or commonwealth and may not be claimed as a personal possession by any individual or any group of individuals not constituting the entire citizenry.* This does not mean communism Bill, not by any means. We are only talking about the ownership of natural resources here. An individual under Lemurian Law may accumulate other assets as long as he has fully compensated for them." Raymond paused for several seconds before continuing "Of course this law and all the other laws are in harmony with the golden rule."

"Christ's golden rule!" Bill exclaimed.

"Exactly, Christ's commandment to love your neighbour as yourself or treat others as we would have them treat us can be expressed in another way as the law of action and reaction, sometimes known as the law of karma."

"We reap what we sow" Bill added.

"Yes" Raymond smiled "If only we would all live by this law the world would be a much better place."

"So you think that the law of karma is the same as the Golden Rule?" Bill asked looking puzzled.

"Essentially yes it is the same. Christ expressed it in many ways so that we might understand it. He also said "with the measure you use it will be measured back to you. And why do you look at the speck in your brother's eye, but do not consider the plank in your own eye?"

"Give and it will be given to you" Sarah whispered. She had perked up again at the talk of Christ, having been raised a devout Christian.

"Precisely" Raymond agreed.

"It's interesting that you compare the Eastern philosophy of karma with these Christian teachings" Bill commented. "Sometimes Christians get freaked out when I talk to them about karma, like it's some forbidden foreign concept."

Raymond grinned "And not just Christians. People of all faiths are frightened to listen to the principles and beliefs of others. Often the concepts are the same, just different language, stories and expressions. The law of karma is basically the same as the Christian concepts of sin and virtue."

Bill nodded "No doubt there is much in common between all faiths, but there are differences between your faith and mainstream Christianity are there not? Such as the idea of reincarnation we discussed before. What other key differences are there between the Lemurian philosophy and mainstream Christianity?"

Raymond scratched his chin thoughtfully "We have an understanding about evolution that differs from the mainstream. We believe that the earth's creatures were evolved to the point where there was an ape suitable for the introduction of our human souls."

"So your views don't conflict with the scientific view of evolution?" Bill interrupted.

"No not really, except that most scientists believe it all happened by chance which is a ridiculous notion."

Bill nodded his agreement "So how did the souls of man get into the evolved apes?"

Raymond smiled "That's a bit like asking how God created the universe, something we can only speculate upon. The event wherein a fixed number of human souls were made ready to take on the bodies of the species known as *Homo sapiens* is called the "fall" of man."

"Yes I've heard of that" Bill responded. "That fixed number must have been more than the number of humans who are alive on the planet today then?"

"Of course, there are always a variable number of human souls who are waiting on the astral plain of existence to be reincarnated, depending on the number of people currently alive."

Bill nodded "How else does the Lemurian Philosophy differ from other forms of Christianity?"

"Another key difference is in the idea of salvation. Many Christians believe that Christ is coming back to *save* us. But if that were true, you'd have to ask why He didn't save us last time He came. Instead He taught us the way to live our lives in order to save ourselves. It doesn't suit many mainstream religions to teach this philosophy because their continued existence relies on people coming to them for salvation."

"Yeah, be initiated into *our* group, it's the *easy* way to salvation" Bill said sarcastically. "That method has been used to attract followers by religious leaders ever since mankind began."

"Yes, but it hasn't always turned out badly" Raymond sighed. He seemed now to be growing slightly impatient.

Bill looked at Sarah and, from many years of being together, he was able to glean from her expression that she thought it was time to leave.

"We mustn't hold you up any longer Raymond. Thank you for the fascinating discussion."

"You're welcome" Raymond responded warmly. "I have also enjoyed our chat. I'll give you a brochure and some of our introductory materials, in case you would like to think about enrolment in the course."

"Thanks I'll certainly give it some thought" Bill replied. They thanked Raymond again and left.

"What did you think of him?" Bill asked as they headed back to the highway.

"He seems very sincere" Sarah replied.

Bill nodded "I was hoping he would tell us more about the origins of the Lemurian Philosophy. He said that the Brotherhoods gave the ideas to Stelle but he didn't elaborate much and he didn't mention Zitco at all."

Bill was referring to Howard John Zitco, who, according to Bill's research on the internet, had been the cofounder of the Lemurian Fellowship.

"You didn't ask him about Zitco though" Sarah pointed out.

"I guess I was a bit afraid to because they never seem to mention him in their literature. Hopefully we'll find out more about Zitco at the next destination."

It was towards Zitco's headquarters in Benson Arizona that they were now headed. Although Zitco himself had died in 2003 at the ripe old age of 92, his legacy was "The World University" purporting to offer courses in esoteric spiritual consciousness.

It was a full day's drive from Ramona to Benson. Bill and Sarah were glad to arrive at the cheap but comfortable Arizona motel. Bill asked the receptionist if she knew where the World University was. "The world what?" was the bewildered reply, "Never heard of it."

"That seems strange" Bill remarked to Sarah. "Benson is only a small place; you'd think they would know." There was no address on the internet, but Sarah stumbled on an old directory in the motel room and fortunately found an address.

Bill was excited as he set the GPS for Desert Sanctuary Road and they headed for the foothills of the Rincon mountain range. The landscape was rugged, hot, harsh desert country. An old sign pointed to "WORLD UNIVERSITY—Desert Sanctuary Campus." It was full of bullet holes. Interestingly there were several signs marking other properties, none of which had been shot up. "They can't be very popular" Bill chuckled as they turned in the direction of the sign.

The road became progressively worse until it was virtually impassable. The gravel surface diminished until there was almost pure sand. Bill nearly lost control of the car trying to dodge enormous potholes, at the same time as maintaining enough speed so as not to get stuck in the sand.

Finally they arrived at a car park outside a forbidding looking fence, with a sign saying "Beware of rattlesnakes." The grass was overgrown and it all seemed neglected and deserted, exuding a strong sense of foreboding. "It's a complete contrast to Ramona" Sarah remarked as Bill got out of the car to investigate.

Bill apprehensively opened the gate into the front yard. It looked rather pretty despite being unkempt and Bill imagined that it must have been magnificent at one time. There was a large swimming pool adjacent, empty and neglected. A sign over the front door read "Secretariat visitor centre." Bill knocked on the door several times, without success. There was no sign of activity and Bill peered through the window. It looked like simple living quarters, certainly not a "visitor centre", let alone a university.

"Whatever this once might have been, it must have died with Zitco." Bill shook his head sadly as he got back into the car with Sarah. "I don't think there's anything to learn here." Bill drove off in silence, a little disappointed in having come so far with so little to show for it.

"At least we know now" Sarah commented, "what it's like."

After a few minutes Bill nodded "At least we can concentrate on our holiday now." The next destination of interest for Bill's book was more than halfway across the USA near Chicago and they had planned to see some of the sites on their way across. And so they did. They visited the wondrous Grand Canyon, before traversing the spectacular Rocky Mountains. They were thoroughly impressed by the magnificence of the countryside and the friendliness of the people. They journeyed over the vast Great Plains and cornfields of the Midwest, and crossed the mighty Mississippi before finally approaching their destination.

They had obtained the coordinates from the Internet and set their GPS, but as they neared the destination Bill began to wonder if they had the wrong location. They were right in the middle of vast fields planted to soybeans and corn, seemingly as far as the eye could see in all directions. Then suddenly they saw the entrance, an attractive sign that said simply: "Stelle." A neat driveway led into a maze of streets with beautiful houses nestled amongst immaculate gardens and lawns. The scene would look fitting in an affluent suburb of any town in America. Only in this case it seemed bizarre, almost surreal. The suburb was not in a town but in the middle of the crop fields.

"This is Kieninger's town" Bill said. "The one inspired by "The Ultimate Frontier"."

Sarah nodded; she knew the significance of this place to Bill. They drove down all the streets, seeing no signs of life other than some cars parked on the street. Bill stopped at a building signposted as a community centre but it was locked. As he returned to the car, a vehicle pulled up and parked outside one of the adjacent houses. An elderly man got out with bags of groceries.

"Excuse me sir" Bill asked politely "I wonder if you can help me?"

"Yes" the man approached them, still holding his groceries, "What can I do for you?"

"I'm interested in your community" Bill explained. "I read "The Ultimate Frontier" many years ago and as we are passing through on our way across America I wondered what had happened to it all."

The old man laughed "That *was* a long time ago. We don't get much interest in that aspect any more. These days we just have a quiet little community here. Richard Kieninger isn't very popular around here you know and most of the people who were associated with him have long since left. He hasn't been welcome here for 30 years and I believe he went through transition back in 2002."

These words were familiar to Bill. "Transition" was a word that meant death to those of the Lemurian faith. "Were you one of the original members of Stelle?" he asked.

"Actually yes I was. I'll tell you what, I need to put these groceries away but I could offer you a cup of coffee if you like?"

Sarah smiled "Thank you that would be lovely."

"My name is Chris" he said as he motioned for them to sit at his kitchen table while he put his groceries away.

"Pleased to meet you, I'm Bill and this is my wife Sarah. So how long have you lived in Stelle?"

"Since the 1970s, not long after it first started" Chris replied. Richard Kieninger turned out to be a louse but there were lots of good things he did for us; especially in the early days. First of all he inspired us to build this community from nothing and that in itself was a great achievement. Also the fact that we had people here from all different backgrounds living in peace and harmony was wonderful. It's still a nice place to live. A bit of a drive to get provisions though" he added as he put the last of his groceries away.

"But unfortunately the peace and harmony didn't last" he continued. "In fact Richard was responsible for breaking up a lot of marriages around here, including mine." Chris shook his head with obvious annoyance.

"Sorry to hear that" Bill sympathised. "We heard about his womanising and so on. I'm interested to know about the origins of the ideas that went into "The Ultimate Frontier". Do you know how much was taken directly from the Lemurian Fellowship's course material?"

Chris nodded "Pretty much word for word really. I did get to see a copy of the Lemurian course material, and from what I can gather, all he did was to write himself into the story as the "chosen one" and put dates on the predicted upheavals, such as Armageddon."

"So do you think he was ever in touch with the Brotherhoods and do you believe they even exist?"

"Good question" Chris replied. "I honestly don't know the answer to that. I do believe they exist but I can't prove it to you. Of course we all thought Richard was in touch with the Brotherhoods in the early days, but then we finally cottoned on to his lies. After that I suppose we couldn't really believe anything he said. At one stage I think he was in touch with Zitco when he claimed to be receiving information from the Brotherhoods."

Bill interrupted "You mean Howard John Zitco, the cofounder of the Lemurian fellowship?"

"Yes, you know about him?" Chris raised his eyebrows.

"Only what I've read on the Internet" Bill replied. "What can you tell me about him?"

"I can tell you that he was indeed the cofounder of the Lemurian Fellowship. He and Robert Stelle apparently had a falling out in the early days of the Lemurian Fellowship and Zitco went his own way, offering a similar course of study through his so-called World University.

I did meet him myself back in the 1980s. In my opinion he was not a very nice man, seemed to be utterly self-absorbed, narcissistic even. Surprisingly he was into all the spiritualism and occult stuff that Richard was so dead set against. Maybe the Black Mentalists got to him, maybe they got to Richard too in the end . . ." Chris seemed to drift off into thought.

"What do you know of the original material that Zitco and Stelle put together? What was the source of that?" Bill asked.

"Still something of a mystery I'm afraid" Chris responded. "There are conflicting accounts, but Zitco himself told me the ideas were "channelled" through Stelle. According to him, Stelle would slip into a trance and Zitco would write down the words he spoke in his sleep."

"Sounds like Edgar Cayce or Muhammad" Bill suggested.

"Yes, I suppose so" Chris replied.

"What happened to the partnership between Stelle and Zitco?" Bill continued.

"Well that's an interesting story you know. As I understand it, Stelle saw himself as the character Rhu and Zitco as Hut in his book "The Sun Rises." There does seem to be a strong resemblance between the Rhu and Hut story and the story of Stelle and Zitco. I mean in the way they collaborated initially in building a civilisation and then fell out. Hut's fall from grace seems to mirror the way that Zitco fell out of favour with Stelle. The personalities of the two men also seem to match those described of Rhu and Hut, though I suppose it depends on who is telling the story . . ." Chris paused.

"That is interesting" Bill agreed "especially when you consider what's happened to their respective followings since their deaths. Stelle has a devoted group of followers who continue to "keep the faith" and to deliver the course material more than half a century after his death. On the other hand Zitco's enterprise appears to have decayed away to nothing within a few years of his death."

"Is that right? Chris asked. "I haven't heard what happened to either organisation for many years."

"Yes we recently visited both" Bill responded.

Chris nodded reflectively "I guess you could say that Richard went the same way as Zitco. The Stelle Group no longer exits."

"Didn't Richard start a new group down in Texas though?" Bill interrupted.

Chris nodded "Yes, he formed the Adelphi organisation after he was expelled from here. They continue to publish his books. They're a small group of die-hard followers that never saw through him."

"But don't you think his works still have value?" Bill suggested.

"I guess so" Chris conceded. "I must confess that despite all Richard's lies and so on, I remain grateful for the philosophy he introduced me to. I'm still pretty much a believer in the Lemurian Philosophy. It's given me a lasting faith and has helped me a great deal in my life."

"It's helped Bill too" Sarah, who had been listening intently, finally remarked.

Bill nodded his acknowledgement "But I like to remain a free agent" he declared. "The Lemurian philosophy is good but it doesn't have the whole Truth. I'm wary nowadays of any group or individual that says they have the absolute Truth or that they are in touch with God or "ascended masters"."

"Or the Brotherhoods" Chris smiled.

"Yeah" Bill agreed. "When you think about it though, that's what's behind pretty well all cults and religions. There's always someone who claims to have a "connection" with higher powers. It's easy to be sucked in by someone who claims, with great self-confidence and conviction that they know the absolute Truth because they've been told it by God or another higher being."

Chris nodded "Does it really matter though?" he queried. "In the end we'll probably never know the whole truth about these matters. The three men we've been talking about are all departed now and they have taken their secrets with them. What matters really is the philosophy itself and whether it's right for us at the present time."

"I suppose so" Bill conceded, "although I personally would like to know the real Truth. I mean there is only one Truth in the end.

Maybe one day we'll have only one religion that's based on the real Truth."

Chris shook his head "I don't think that's very likely in the foreseeable future. There is only one Truth but it's not possible at the present time to contain the whole truth in one religion. If there was only one religion it could get taken over by bad or misguided men, then where would we be?"

"You could be right there" Bill agreed. "That argument could also be applied to the world's nations. If we ended up with a world government, along the lines of what some UN people seem to be advocating, and the leadership fell into the wrong hands . . . well it doesn't bear thinking about."

"Yes, it's probably a good thing to have a diversity of sects and religions" Chris concurred. "Even a sect that starts out righteously can become corrupted by rotten people who take over the leadership."

"Like Richard" Bill chuckled.

Chris roared with laughter "I don't know if Richard was ever righteous."

They sat in silence momentarily. Bill glanced at Sarah and stood up to leave. They warmly thanked Chris for his hospitality and promised to get in touch by email on their return home.

As they made their way back into the cornfields of Illinois Sarah reflected "Isn't it amazing how in such a short space of time the Lemurian Philosophy has broken into four schisms?"

"It sure is" Bill agreed "But like Chris said, maybe that's a good thing. Imagine if Zitco had taken control of the Lemurian Fellowship after Stelle's death. The whole thing might have ended up at that dead end in the Desert.

Also when a religion breaks into schisms it's pretty hard to figure out who are the good guys and who are the bad guys. Maybe the good guys become the bad guys and vice versa. They change over time. People come and go, splits happen over dogma and the egos of the leaders and the group may go closer or further from the Truth."

Sarah nodded "If that can happen to such a small group in only 50 years, imagine what can happen on a bigger scale. Like the

Christian Church over two thousand years. It's easy to see how we have such a multitude of schisms and offshoots."

"Yeah" Bill replied "and figuring out which one has the Truth is a big problem."

Chapter 3—The Deist

"We hold these Truths to be self evident, that all Men are created equal, that they are endowed by their Creator with certain unalienable Rights, that among these are Life, Liberty and the pursuit of Happiness." The Declaration of Independence.

Bill and Sarah's next planned destination was Washington DC but they were in no hurry to get there. They spent two nights at the glorious Niagara Falls and several days in picturesque upstate New York, which was a spectacular sea of green interrupted by blazes of reds, yellows and stunning bright orange autumn colours.

This was followed by several days in New York City, the highlight of which was a visit to "ground zero" the site that once housed the twin towers of the World Trade Centre. Although it had been nearly a decade since that shocking day, it was still very raw in the hearts and minds of the people who had lost loved ones. On the other hand however, the majority of New York's people had moved on with the business of living in this great city.

Their arrival in Washington DC was to coincide with a date that had been arranged by Hamish. On hearing Bill's travel plans, Hamish had strongly recommended a visit to his friend Simon in Washington. They had a day to spare before the planned rendezvous so they visited the sights of the city. Bill was impressed by the wide streets and the majestic buildings boasting facades of columns, arches and decoration. "It looks like I imagine the city of ancient Rome would have looked" Bill remarked.

"Similarities in its status in the world too" Sarah suggested. "It's the centre of our modern civilisation in the same way that Rome was the centre in its day."

Bill nodded as they walked along Pennsylvania Avenue. They took the obligatory photos of each other in front of the Whitehouse before heading out onto the expansive parkland leading to the Washington Monument. From there they could admire the immaculate layout of the city. To the east the National Mall hemmed with its museums and galleries led to the US Capitol. To the west the beautiful reflecting pool traced a perfect straight line through Memorial Park towards the enigmatic Lincoln Memorial building.

They strolled through Memorial Park, admiring the gardens, fountains and monuments. They read the inscriptions immortalising great words from the past that continued to resonate the ideals of this proud country: Liberty and Justice. As Bill read the words etched into a wall "Freedom is not free" he felt a wave of emotion wash over him. "Still so true" he murmured. He looked around and saw that Sarah had walked on ahead towards the Lincoln Memorial. Bill however, was drawn to the right where there stood an incredibly lifelike statue of three soldiers in full battle kit, in memorial of the Vietnam War.

Bill drifted into thought as he stood beside these three soldiers. He imagined for a moment he could hear the sounds of battle. He followed the gaze of the soldiers, towards the lists of men killed in action in Vietnam. This memorial meant more to Bill than the others, for these men were of Bill's generation, young men in the prime of their lives sent to fight in an unpopular war, young men who could have been his mates. He looked up and caught the eyes of another man who had also come over to look at the statue. The man was also caught up in the emotion of the setting, his eyes glistened as he returned Bill's crumpled smile and the two men nodded their mutual acknowledgement of this brief yet powerful shared moment.

Bill rubbed his eyes as he finally moved on to catch up with Sarah who was now inside the Lincoln Memorial building. She smiled, as Bill entered the building, pointing to the words of the Gettysburg address reading it quietly but audibly to Bill:

"Four score and seven years ago our fathers brought forth on this continent, a new nation, conceived in Liberty, and dedicated to the proposition that all men are created equal.

Now we are engaged in a great civil war, testing whether that nation, or any nation so conceived and so dedicated, can long endure. We are met on a great battlefield of that war. We have come to dedicate a portion of that field, as a final resting place for those who here gave their lives that that nation might live. It is altogether fitting and proper that we should do this.

But, in a larger sense, we cannot dedicate—we cannot consecrate—we cannot hallow—this ground. The brave men, living and dead, who struggled here, have consecrated it, far above our poor power to add or detract. The world will little note, nor long remember what we say here, but it can never forget what they did here. It is for us the living, rather, to be dedicated here to the unfinished work which they who fought here have thus far so nobly advanced. It is rather for us to be here dedicated to the great task remaining before us—that from these honored dead we take increased devotion to that cause for which they gave the last full measure of devotion—that we here highly resolve that these dead shall not have died in vain—that this nation, under God, shall have a new birth of freedom—and that government of the people, by the people, for the people, shall not perish from the earth."

"Well he was wrong about one thing" Bill whispered.

"What's that?" Sarah asked.

"That the world will little note, nor long remember what he said. That's the most famous two minute speech in history."

"You're right there" Sarah agreed. "It's a good example of how a few well chosen words can have such a great impact."

Bill nodded "yeah, also an example of a truly great man I think."

They spent the rest of the day exploring more of the city. The following morning, as expected, Bill received an early phone call from Hamish's friend. He had sounded very friendly on the phone. "My name is Simon" he said in a broad American accent. "I've been looking forward to meeting you. Hamish has told me so much about you. I'll meet you on the steps to the Supreme Court opposite the US Capitol building at 9am" he said.

Bill had no idea what to expect but thought it best to ask Sarah if she wouldn't mind staying at the hotel that morning. She smiled and said that she had lots of postcards and emails to attend to and was glad to get some time to herself.

Bill arrived at the rendezvous shortly before 9am. He was somewhat apprehensive about the meeting. All Hamish had told him was that it was important that he meet with Simon. Bill was deep in thought, admiring the magnificent Capitol building, which appeared to be undergoing renovations, when a voice greeted him "Good morning Bill, thanks for coming!"

Bill looked up to see a man about his own age, well dressed in a dark suit extending his hand. "You must be Simon" Bill responded as he shook hands warmly with the smiling gentleman.

"That's right; it's wonderful to meet you at last. We're going on a short car ride if that's OK with you. There are some people I'd like you to meet."

"Sure" Bill stammered. This was starting to get interesting. Meet some people, what people? he wondered.

Just then a black SUV with heavily tinted windows pulled up next to them and Simon beckoned Bill to get in the back with him. As soon as the door was shut Simon looked at Bill, his expression now more serious. "I'm afraid I'm going to ask you to put on a blindfold, just for a few minutes. My colleagues like to keep their meeting place a secret."

"OK" Bill replied hesitantly. The situation was getting a little scary. He hadn't worn a blindfold since he was a child. However he trusted Hamish implicitly and felt he had no choice but to comply. Hamish wouldn't have sent him to meet bad people.

Simon assisted Bill in wrapping the dark coloured cloth around his eyes. The vehicle had by now moved out into the traffic. Bill could not see a thing.

"Don't worry" Simon said reassuringly "it's just a formality."

Bill tried to hide his anxiety with a smile. "No worries, it reminds me of playing blind man's bluff."

It seemed only a few minutes later that the vehicle came to a stop. "It's OK you can take that off now" Simon said.

The door was opened by the driver, a young man who greeted Bill politely as he disembarked. They were in some kind of basement garage where there were several other vehicles parked. There was no view to the outside world, just an elevator into which Simon now beckoned him.

"After the meeting I'd like to take you on a tour of the Capitol building" Simon offered as they went up in the elevator. "I'd like that" Bill replied. "Can we go to the Library of Congress too? I'm researching for a book and I need to know something about American history."

"You've come to the right place" Simon grinned. "The right person too, American history is my specialty."

The elevator opened and they stepped out into a corridor with no signage, just a door at which Simon waved an electronic key and entered, beckoning Bill to follow. The door opened into what looked like a boardroom with a large rectangular table. Around the table sat a group of about a dozen people, mainly men, who all looked up and smiled warmly as Simon spoke. "This is Bill, the gentleman from Australia we've been expecting."

Simon took a vacant seat at the head of the table and motioned for Bill to take the seat next to him. Bill's mind was racing, who were these people?

"You're probably wondering what this is all about" Simon continued as if reading Bill's mind. "We are an organisation dedicated to upholding the values and aspirations of the founding fathers of the United States of America. It is our sworn duty to ensure that America remains strong and continues to be a force for freedom and democracy in the world. We think of ourselves as a watchdog on the rulers of America.

The founding fathers had a vision for America that was enshrined in the Declaration of Independence and the Constitution. However there are forces that seek to destroy this great vision. Politicians come and go, and while most have the best interests of the USA and its people at heart, some are misguided and seek to bring in laws that restrict the great freedoms and rights of the individual laid down by our forefathers. It often starts benignly by politicians who believe it's their role to bring "social justice" to the world, but that develops into a desire to dictate how others should lead their lives. It's our job to monitor any such threats and to do anything we can to prevent them from gaining a foothold."

"How do you do that?" Bill asked politely.

"We prefer not to talk about our methods" Simon replied. "Suffice to say that we work through normal channels of influence. There's nothing sinister in what we do. We just like our organisation to remain secret, for obvious reasons."

"I understand" Bill nodded.

Simon continued "The reason we were anxious to talk to you is that we believe you are involved in a similar group in your own country."

Bill was surprised. Had Hamish disclosed the existence of the Junto to Simon? Was the Junto perhaps even connected with this organisation? "What did Hamish tell you?" he stammered apprehensively.

Simon grinned "Don't worry we won't blow your cover. We will respect your right to secrecy as I'm sure you will respect ours. Hamish has been our only contact with your group until now. However we believe it's important that we talk to you now. We're concerned about a number of things happening in the USA that you are also dealing with in Australia. We are especially interested in the work you've been doing to counter the environmental movement that we believe is an insidious threat to America and even to Western civilisation."

Bill smiled, now it all made sense "Thank you, it will be my pleasure to give you my perspective on this" he responded. "This issue is indeed a serious problem in my country, particularly in regard to the so-called "climate change" debate. The current Government is attempting to bring in a tax on carbon dioxide under the belief that man-made carbon dioxide is harming the planet. The scientists who dreamed up this nonsense are in cahoots with the left wing Government that sees this as an opportunity to scare the people. The headline-seeking media is also on the bandwagon, conjuring up doomsday scenarios saying if we don't immediately act to curb our carbon dioxide emissions we will destroy the planet for our grandchildren. The groupthink shoots down dissenters and makes out that anyone who doesn't agree with them is immoral. Climate change sceptics are labelled deniers to liken them to holocaust deniers. Carbon dioxide is called pollution . . . it makes me sick!" Bill hesitated. He had begun to get quite emotional and suddenly became conscious of the intensity with which his audience were listening. "Sorry if I am getting a little carried away."

"No problem at all" Simon smiled. "What you've explained is happening here too. Perhaps not to the same extent but we intend to make sure it doesn't go that far. This is precisely the kind of thing we are here to guard against. This herd mentality you talk about is a significant threat. When irrational ideas become the norm, when dissenters are ostracised and prevented from expressing their views, evil can spread this way and take over entire countries, as we have seen for example in Nazi Germany. But do go on."

"Thanks" Bill continued. "Funny you should mention the Nazis, because it's occurred to me that the modern environmental movement has a lot in common with Nazi ideology. They have similar ideas about nature, ideas that elevate animals to the level of people, or even above people, maintaining that humans are a threat to the planet. Environmentalism has become the new atheist religion."

Simon interrupted "Yes and the saddest thing is that these people believe they are the good guys. Ordinary people are caught up in the mass hysteria. Make no mistake though, this movement is not harmless. If these people are allowed to have their way they will destroy our civilisation. What are you doing to counter this in Australia?"

Bill went on to explain the work that he and others were doing through the Science Junto in opposition to the new green political force. He answered several questions from other members of the group, all of whom seemed keenly interested and were appreciative of Bill's answers. "You can't fight this kind of thing in an overt conventional political debate. The media won't let you. It's a covert war" Bill concluded.

This prompted a round of applause and Simon thanked Bill for his insights and wound up the meeting. Bill soon found himself alone with Simon retracing the journey back to the outside world. True to his word Simon took Bill on a fascinating tour of the US

Capitol building. It was apparent that Simon worked there as he had a security pass that seemed to allow him access throughout, though Bill wasn't able to figure out what his position was.

Simon had not exaggerated his knowledge of US history. He spoke passionately and in detail about the foundation of the nation. As agreed the tour ended at the Thomas Jefferson Building, part of the Library of Congress. There were more questions that Bill wanted to ask so Simon suggested they go to a small meeting room where they could get a coffee and talk in private.

"So what else do you want to know?" Simon asked as they sat down with their coffees.

"Well, the book I'm researching for is about religion. I'd like to find out about the religious views of the founding fathers. Did they have a common philosophy and did that have any bearing on the founding of the USA?"

Simon nodded thoughtfully "Well of course they were a diverse group, but the man with the most influence and who drafted the Declaration of Independence was Thomas Jefferson. He was a Deist, as was Benjamin Franklin, along with a number of others. That was the philosophy perhaps most influential on the founding documents. The Deists believed that God created the universe and its laws, but they believed that the laws operate perfectly on their own without any continuing intervention from God. They argued that if God needed to intervene all the time it would imply that His original laws weren't perfect. And that wouldn't make sense if we accept that God is the all-knowing perfect being."

"So they didn't think God needed to intervene with miracles then?" Bill suggested.

"No, but at the same time, they believed that the existence of the perfect laws bringing order to the universe proves the very existence of God. The laws themselves are the miracle."

"So they definitely weren't atheists then?"

"Oh no, absolutely not!" Simon exclaimed. The laws of physics and chemistry convinced them utterly that there was indeed a Creator God. To them it was as plain as day that the laws of the universe were designed by a creative force. Jefferson and his colleagues were so convinced of this logic that they would have thought anyone stupid to believe otherwise."

Bill nodded "Why do you think modern scientists don't see this logic?"

"I don't know, to me it's a very convincing argument. The laws of physics and so on are so perfect that it makes no sense that they happened by chance. I guess it's a case of modern scientists throwing the baby out with the bath water, like you said in your book."

"You've read my book about science?" Bill was surprised.

"Yes, we all have, it's very poignant."

"Thank you" Bill blushed. "It's been a passion of mine. The stupidity of modern science blinded by its own dogma never ceases to amaze me."

"Quite right" Simon agreed. "Of course Franklin and Jefferson were scientists themselves in a sense. They thought the scientific method was the ideal means for discovering the truth. Jefferson hated religious dogma that professed to be the absolute Truth just because it appeared in a certain book; or if it was claimed to be true because it was supposedly "revealed" to someone claiming to be a prophet of God. He rejected any theology that made no sense to him such as the Trinity, which he said he didn't understand. He said that if you didn't understand something then why would you believe in it?"

"That's a good point" Bill acknowledged. "The Trinity has never made any sense to me either. And isn't it funny how the people who most believe in some nonsense are often the ones who least understand it and are also the ones who push the idea the most?"

"Like the belief in man-made global warming" Simon chuckled. "Your point was well made this morning that belief in man-made global warming is akin to the dogma of an organised religion. Climate science has become a religion with the climate scientists its priests, the media its henchmen and the public its ignorant congregation who fail to question the prevailing authority."

"Yes and the fact the government has adopted it as their policy means it's become the religion of the State too" Bill grinned.

"There's no separation of religion from State when it comes to the environmental religion."

"Good point" Simon laughed. "Jefferson would be appalled at what has become of modern science and the abandonment of the scientific method. He despised the alliances that existed between European priests and kings that kept each other in power, each reliant on the other to maintain their authority. The way they kept their subjects in a state of unthinking moral dependence is similar to what's happening today. Scientists are the unchallenged arbiters of the Truth and maintain their alliance with the politicians who are too frightened to challenge the prevailing dogma. Any challenge to the authority of science is shot down by the morally bankrupt media."

"Yeah" Bill nodded "priests of all religions dislike those who undermine their authority. Christ Himself struggled against the religious leaders of His day. How did Jefferson get away with his criticism of the Churches?"

"That's an interesting question, of course he did have his conflicts with some Church leaders, but he was able to negotiate his way through the minefield of religious authority by promoting the idea of separation of Church and State. This was an idea that already had some traction through the writings of John Locke and others. Above all he wanted to ensure that no individual sect was able to gain control of the State. He was lucky there were already a number of rival denominations in America and none had yet become dominant as had occurred in Europe. Jefferson was very conscious of the fact that virtually all religions and sects believed that theirs was the one and only absolute Truth. Therefore if any one of them was allowed to dominate, then real truth would inevitably be suppressed."

"He was very wise" Bill concurred.

"Furthermore" Simon continued, "Jefferson thought that religious dogma was the enemy of reason. If your reason conflicted with any aspect of your sect's dogma then you were obliged either to reject your reason or leave the sect. Any deviation was considered heresy."

"Heresy" Bill repeated "a crime sometimes punishable by death, even today in some religions. Things haven't changed much." He paused to make some notes. "So if Jefferson didn't accept any dogma, where did his ideas about morality come from?"

Simon scratched his chin thoughtfully "Jefferson believed that reason alone could determine all moral questions of right and wrong. He believed that all God's Laws could be empirically discovered by man through his power of reason and observation. This held as true for Universal Laws covering morality as it did for the laws of physics."

"But didn't Jefferson believe in Christian morality though?" Bill interrupted.

"Yes I suppose he did" Simon agreed. "Jefferson was a great believer in the morality of Christ and the lessons He left for us. He even made his own abbreviated version of the New Testament that cuts out much dogma and anything he thought was contradictory or didn't make sense. He thought that the lessons of Christ could be reduced to a few simple moral truths. In a letter to John Adams he said Christ's lessons were the most sublime and benevolent code of morals which has ever been offered to man and that these simple Truths were as easily distinguishable as diamonds in a dunghill.

Bill laughed "Diamonds in a dunghill that's a good one! Really interesting though, because that's exactly what I'm finding in my own research; that the lessons of Christianity can be distilled in this way. So obviously he didn't reject the teachings of Christ then?"

"No, only if they conflicted with his sense of reason. Above all he believed in the first principle of Christ's teaching: to love your neighbour as yourself. He believed that many of the other moral laws could be derived from this."

"Such as do not murder, steal, commit adultery and so on" Bill suggested.

"Exactly" Simon agreed, "Jefferson thought that all the complex theological dogma was put there by the priesthood to make sure we require them to explain it. If it was just a case of a few simple moral truths there would be no need for priests."

"That's so true!" Bill laughed. "Were there any particular parts of the Bible that he particularly disliked?"

"He was especially critical of the writings of Paul."

"Me too!" Bill exclaimed. "I reckon a lot of orthodox Christianity should be called Paulianity. It's always been a mystery to me that a man like Paul, who never even knew Christ, had such a major impact on Christian theology."

Simon nodded "I guess Paul was a good organizer, a charismatic figure and maybe he imposed his preconceived ideas on the religion. But Paul's doctrines weren't the only ones Jefferson had a problem with. Along with other Deists he was averse to the idea of predestination that was part of much Christian theology."

"Yeah it makes no sense to me either" Bill agreed. "The idea that we're predestined to salvation or damnation is crazy, it would make God unjust. If we are predestined, then what would be the point of being good? If God is just then our individual behaviour must affect our ultimate reward or punishment."

"Yes I agree" Simon nodded. "I guess the idea of predestination was needed to explain the perceived injustice of inequality that appears to exist in the world."

"My belief in reincarnation and karma accounts for that problem" Bill responded.

"Yes I guess it does. I don't know if the Deists had considered reincarnation, but it wouldn't be inconsistent with their philosophy. They believed there were universal laws that provide for an appropriate reward and punishment for our behaviour either in this life or the next. They also believed that whatever system existed would have to be fair, so that the degree of reward or punishment would be commensurate with the degree of good or bad done by the individual."

"And the heaven versus hell idea doesn't meet that criteria" Bill interjected "whereas the concepts of karma and reincarnation do."

"Yes I suppose so" Simon acknowledged. "But the Deists generally chose not to speculate on matters that couldn't be proven. The main thing they believed is that salvation was not granted by God's grace or to any arbitrary sect but is earned by good works. It was up to each individual to find his own path to salvation. Jefferson would never submit himself to any one creed because if he did so he would be giving religious authority precedence over reason."

"OK" Bill offered "so I guess that's why he was keen to ensure freedom of religion."

"Yes, but also in encouraging religious freedom, he thought that in an open society where people were free to discuss and debate religious matters, that eventually reason would prevail and consequently the real truth would overtake the nonsense. He envisaged a single religion of Truth emerging from the debate."

"That's interesting" Bill remarked. "But that hasn't happened though has it? Instead of a single religion of truth, we have yet more schisms each professing that theirs is the one true way at the exclusion of others."

"I guess so" Simon conceded. "Jefferson thought that if people were given the right of free speech, then there would be open debates about theology. Perhaps this hasn't happened because it's not in the interests of priests and other religious leaders. Their positions of power can only be maintained if the dogma is maintained. Open debate isn't encouraged on the grounds that it's disrespectful to criticise another's religious views."

"Tell me about it" Bill responded emphatically. "These days even so-called "good" religious leaders are often apologists for some bloody awful religions. They sympathise with rival religions because they fear that reasoned examination of any religious philosophy will lead to exposing the shortcomings in their own dogma. We've developed this modern politically correct relativist system where all religions are equal and there's no debate over Truth."

"It does seem a sad state of affairs" Simon agreed, "but at least we don't have the religious bigotry, intolerance and hatred that occur in other parts of the world. In America we have a multitude of religions and ethnic groups living in peace alongside each other. What we have in common is our love for freedom of the individual, justice and democracy. We share the vision of our founding fathers who believed in working together to build this great land of opportunity, where its citizens could achieve reward for hard work and enterprise."

Simon was getting quite animated, the passion showing in his voice. Bill sensed something of the patriotism that was common in America. He also noticed that Simon was starting to look at his watch. He said "Simon, thank you very much for your time. You've been marvellous."

"You're very welcome Bill, glad to be of service. I do have to get going but I'd be glad to talk to you some more, do you have any more spare time while you are in the US?"

"Yes we have a few days up our sleeve."

"Well I have an idea. I heard a rumour that you like to fish for trout."

"You heard right" Bill grinned.

"Well my brother runs a ranch in Wyoming, nearby some of the best fishing in the USA. From tomorrow I'll be spending a few days there and you and your wife are welcome to join us if you'd like?"

"I'm sure we'd love to" Bill responded.

Bill said goodbye to Simon who said he would be in touch to discuss arrangements. Bill knew he had to sell the idea of making an unplanned flight to Wyoming to Sarah. However that proved to be no problem when Bill pointed out that their destination was right next to Yellowstone National Park.

Within two days they were landing in the Wild West town of Cody Wyoming, which was the nearest town to Simon's brother's ranch. They were met by Simon's brother Josh, and his wife Nadine who were extremely welcoming and friendly. Because the ranch was some distance out of town they decided that they would firstly eat together at the famous Irma Hotel. They had arrived at exactly the right time to see a gun fight re-enactment outside the hotel, complete with real guns, though thankfully with blanks.

As they sat down at their table they were greeted by a realistic Buffalo Bill lookalike, sporting real six-guns. "You might have noticed there's quite a gun culture around here" Josh said. "We have eight guns for every man woman and child in town and yet we have virtually no crime. Amazing huh?"

They enjoyed the famous Prime Rib buffet amidst the friendly Wild West atmosphere. Over dinner they learned that Josh and Nadine had two grown up sons, one of whom was currently serving in Afghanistan.

After dinner they drove to the ranch and in the morning they rose early as they were all going on a trip to Yellowstone National Park, which was only an hour's drive from the ranch. In the light of day Bill was able to admire the tidy western style ranch with its timber buildings and stockyards, complete with an American flag flying proudly at the entrance.

Yellowstone was magnificent, reminding Bill of the volcanic region in New Zealand where he grew up, though the geysers here were more numerous and much more spectacular. They enjoyed trout for lunch at the grand Lake Yellowstone Hotel and spent the afternoon admiring the spectacular gorges, waterfalls and geothermal features.

The following morning the men set off for two days fishing. Sarah would stay with Nadine who promised to take her to Cody to do some shopping for the family back in Australia.

After a drive through some stunning landscape they arrived at what Josh described as his favourite stretch of the Clarks Fork of Yellowstone River. They made camp which involved pitching a tent before setting out for the day's fishing. Bill was rather apprehensive about bears, which were reportedly quite numerous in the region. When he quizzed Josh about them he was met with a roar of laughter. "Afraid you might get eaten?" he joked. Seeing that Bill didn't look very amused he added more kindly "Don't worry they keep to themselves. They won't bother us if we don't bother them."

However his reassurances didn't really satisfy Bill who spent quite a lot of time looking over his shoulder and made sure he kept fairly close to Josh and Simon. At one point he became separated for a short time but when he saw what looked like a large animal print in the mud he sprinted to quickly catch up with the other men.

The fishing itself turned out to be quite disappointing for Bill. Between them they did catch several trout but Bill thought they were all quite small. He dared not say anything however because he gathered that Simon and Josh thought these fish were just fine. On the other hand the absolutely stunning scenery more than made up for the small fish. All in all, Bill had a fabulous day.

When they arrived back at camp late in the day the temperature was already dropping rapidly. At this altitude of about seven thousand feet the nights were cold even in summer. They built a warm fire and cooked two of the trout they'd caught, which made a nice entrée and enjoyed some of Josh's steaks for the main course.

When they had finished Josh told them to make sure there was no food left lying around that might attract bears. Then they built the fire up and talked and enjoyed some twelve-year-old duty free whiskey that Bill had been keeping for such a fitting occasion.

Both Josh and Simon were quite political and the conversation never drifted far from politics. "Well I like Sarah Palin" Josh said. "Did you hear what she said to Obama in a speech? "We'll keep our religion and our guns and you can keep the change." What a classic!"

Simon grinned, winking at Bill. "The government took your guns away in Australia didn't they?" Josh continued.

Bill replied defensively "Well not exactly. It is much harder to get a gun now though, because of some maniac that killed thirty-five people in one go some years back. The government of the day had a knee-jerk reaction and passed the new gun restrictions."

"That would never happen in Wyoming" Josh said, "because someone would have shot that son-of-a-bitch before he even got to the second victim. I don't think I like your system where only the bad guys and the government have guns. Hell, we hardly have any crime around here because the criminals know they might get shot themselves. In your system an armed robber can do anything he wants because he knows he's going to be the only one with a gun. And if some maniac came into my house and started raping and killing my family, I would rather have a gun handy than be slaughtered like a helpless sheep."

"Forgive my brother's ranting" Simon chipped in. "It's his favourite subject."

"No that's quite alright" Bill responded. "Actually I agree with him. In the USA your gun rights are protected by the second amendment to the constitution. In Australia we have no such protection. We have to rely on the government to protect us."

"And you can't rely on them" Josh interjected. "Hell, one day you might need to fight the government. What's going to happen when things go belly up one day and you don't have guns? You'll be taken over by people who do have guns."

"You could be right" Bill agreed.

"Damn right I'm right and if we don't keep fighting to keep our guns here those left wing intellectuals will take them away from us. If we're not vigilant those decadent liberals will destroy our civilisation too, just like the Greeks, the Romans and every other civilisation that ever existed was destroyed: by their own decadence."

"But we're not going to let that happen are we bro?" Simon punched his brother's shoulder in a friendly way.

"No way, thank God for heartland USA, that's all I can say" Josh concluded.

With that they prepared for bed. Bill was quite nervous about the presence of bears and went into a fitful sleep, clutching his torch in one hand and a utility knife in the other. The next thing he knew, he heard a blood curdling scream. Instinctively his thumb clicked on his torch to reveal the horrific sight that confronted him. The tent had been ripped away and an enormous bear appeared to be mauling Simon. Before he could even think about what to do there was a deafening explosion and the bear slumped over beside Simon. Bill moved his torch to see Josh clutching a smoking handgun.

"That son-of-a-bitch won't do that again" he said "Are you OK bro?"

Simon's voice was shaky but he stammered "Yes I think so, just a scratch on my shoulder, reckon you were just in the nick of time thanks bro."

Josh leaned down to inspect his brother's wound and nodded "Yep I think you'll be fine. Thanks to Bill too. I wouldn't have had that clean shot if you hadn't got that torch on when you did."

Bill's heart was still pounding but he managed a sheepish grin "Thanks, good reflexes I guess. That was good shooting, looks like you blew its brains out" he added. "I didn't even know you had a gun with you."

Josh laughed "Forty-four magnum did the trick. You didn't think I'd come out here with all these bears around without a gun did you?"

"Yeah, I see what you mean now about the gun laws" Bill grinned. "You sure know how to make your point."

Josh chuckled, now looking down to study the carcass of the enormous beast that lay lifeless between them. "Thank God it's a Black" he said. "It could have got complicated if it had been a Grizzly."

"Why is that?" Bill asked.

"Those sons-of-bitches are protected" Josh scoffed, "but God knows why."

Although Simon's wound looked relatively minor, they decided to pack up and get him to hospital to have it checked.

Chapter 4—The Christian

"Doing what's right isn't the problem. It's knowing what's right."
Lyndon B Johnson

Bill and Sarah's trip to the USA had been a great adventure and their homecoming was something of a comedown in comparison. On top of that Bill found he needed to face up to some realities. Their business was in some financial difficulty owing to the global economic downturn and Bill found it necessary to go back into the workforce as an accountant.

He hadn't worked in his old profession for many years and was apprehensive about finding a job. However because of his good past record he was able to secure a position as Financial Manager for a small manufacturing company. After a brief initial period of getting his head back into the accountant mode he started to settle into a new routine. The job was quite challenging and he found himself so engaged in it that he had to put aside other commitments, including his book and most of his work for the Junto.

Bill didn't mind the work itself, it was something he was good at and he felt he was doing something useful while at the same time paying the bills. However the job had two main drawbacks. The first was that there was a significant amount of time away from home. The second was that there was an odd culture in the company that made Bill quite uncomfortable. At first he couldn't quite put his finger on what it was. There seemed to be endless meetings in which staff members talked in jargon that appeared to make sense to them, but was gibberish to Bill. The words used sounded very grandiose, but when Bill tried to analyse what was being said it made no sense.

At one of these meetings Bill raised the issue of the jargon. He had been asked to commit to being "whole and complete" and he asked what this meant. He was astounded at the reaction. Virtually the whole team became very defensive. The boss, who was a fearsome woman, became angry and suggested that if he didn't want to commit to this then he didn't have to be there, and that Bill needed to "get it." Bill needed the money and decided to bite his tongue in future and play along for the time being.

After that particular meeting he was approached by one of the sales managers, a man named Rob who hadn't been with the company very long. He seemed to be familiar with all the jargon but appeared reluctant to participate in it. "I liked what you said in there about the jargon" he said. "You said some things I'd like to say myself but I'm not game enough."

"Thanks" Bill acknowledged "I'm finding it all quite bizarre. It's seems a bit like a cult to me."

Rob laughed "Yes exactly. Have they asked you to go on a Landmark course yet?"

Bill thought for a moment "Well now you come to mention it the boss did say something about me attending a Landmark forum or something like that. I've never heard of it. What's it about?"

Rob shook his head "I'm reluctant to say too much, I need my job, but before you agree to go to it you should do some research into Landmark Education for yourself."

"Is that where all the jargon comes from?" Bill asked.

"Pretty much, yes" Rob replied.

"Have you been to this forum?"

Rob nodded "Yes, as far as I know all the staff have been to it and some are even involved in the more advanced levels of the Landmark courses. I just went to the forum, and I found it very confronting."

"In what way?"

"It's very intense. They shut you in a room for about three days and bombard you with all the jargon and so on from 9am until nearly midnight every day. They only give you one meal break per day, discourage even toilet visits and you basically have no time to think about anything else."

"What happens during these sessions?" Bill asked.

"Well they encourage people to expose their innermost emotions to the group. For example they get people to pour their guilt out about something they feel they've done wrong in the past. They basically get a person to break down in public. To me it seemed quite humiliating for the people singled out. Then they supposedly rebuild the person who is then said to be transformed."

Bill nodded "So I guess this "transformation" process is where they pick up all the jargon."

"Yes."

"That sounds pretty scary Rob. Those techniques like wearing people down, public humiliation and not allowing people to think are all well-known brainwashing methods, used in many cults."

Rob nodded "Yes I think you're right."

"And yet you don't seem to have been brainwashed in the same way as the others" Bill remarked. "I wonder why that is? Unless you really have been and you're just trying to gain my trust before you lure me into the cult" he added jokingly.

Rob roared with laughter "I hope not. I guess when you're brainwashed you don't know you're brainwashed. But seriously I do think I was able to resist it."

"How do you reckon you did that?"

"I don't know really, maybe it's because I'm a Christian. You see some of this stuff challenges my Christian beliefs. For example they make out that life has no meaning and that you can invent your own meaning. You can make your reality any way you want. You just wipe the slate clean, "transform" yourself and start again. Well to me that's rubbish. My life already has meaning and you can't just make up your own rules. The rules are already there. They're given by God."

"This is all quite fascinating, thanks for the warning Rob. I'll certainly do some research of my own. I'd like to talk about this with you more sometime."

"Not a problem" Rob replied. "I heard you and I are on a road trip together next week."

Bill researched the Landmark Education organisation on the internet and found that everything Rob had said was true and more. There were numerous adverse testimonials, even horror stories about this organisation. He resolved to start looking for another job and to tolerate it in the meantime.

The following week's road trip with Rob proved to be quite interesting and enjoyable. The project they were working on meant that they would spend considerable time together, both in the car and over dinner, which gave them the opportunity for several long conversations. It turned out that Rob had married into a Pentecostal Church but had grown up in a devout Presbyterian family. In any case he seemed to be very knowledgeable about the Bible and Bill thought this was a good opportunity to further his research.

Over dinner on the first night away Bill was able to resume his conversation with Rob. "You said the other day that your life has meaning. I'm interested to know what you believe that meaning is."

"Our life has meaning when we have a relationship with God through our Saviour Jesus Christ" Rob replied matter-of-factly.

"So how do we have this relationship with God through Christ?" Bill asked.

"First we must have faith in Christ, accept Him as our saviour and then we follow His commandments and repent of our sins."

"Which commandments?"

"The ones in the Bible."

"All of them?"

"Yes" Rob nodded.

"Does that mean you believe everything in the Bible is true?"

"Of course, you can't pick and choose" Rob responded indignantly.

"But some things in the Bible are contradictory" Bill protested.

"What things?"

"Well for a start the timing of the last supper. In John's gospel it occurs before the Passover whereas in the synoptic gospels it occurs at the Passover."

"I guess it's a matter of interpretation" Rob replied defensively. "It's not important anyway."

Bill decided to change his approach. He felt he was getting into some territory that Rob didn't want to go into. "What do you think is the most important; is it having faith or is it being a good person?" he asked.

"Well both are important. Also it depends on what you mean by a good person."

"How would you define good?" Bill enquired.

"Good is the way of Christ that's taught in the Bible" Rob responded.

"Could you still have the relationship with God if you are a good person but don't believe in Christ the saviour?" Bill asked.

"No, I don't believe so because John 14:6 says that no one comes to the Father except through Me."

"But what about those born somewhere where they don't even know about Christ, how can they be saved?"

Rob looked down into his drink and did not answer.

The arguments seemed to be getting somewhat circular, all relying on the Bible being true. Bill changed the subject again and the conversation drifted back to work. They turned to discussing the merits of their boss. "Well the way I always look at it" Rob stated "is that you know them by their fruits."

After dinner Bill went back to his motel room with much food for thought. He was a little disappointed in the fact that Rob was a fundamentalist. Perhaps he was brainwashed too. I guess we all have our delusions, he thought.

As he got ready for bed Bill opened a drawer to put some of his clothes in and there was the Gideon's Bible. While it wasn't unexpected to find a Bible in a motel room, it startled Bill in the moment and it seemed to beckon him. He picked it up and started to read the New Testament. He had read it before but not for some years.

He found the first part of Matthew's gospel pretty boring and soon found himself nodding off to sleep. "Boy it's no wonder they call this the thousand page sleeping pill" he muttered to himself. But he persevered as far as the Sermon on the Mount when there finally seemed to be some useful material. This is good stuff; he thought to himself, "You will know them by their fruits." That's what Rob said.

It makes sense. Maybe I could sort out the wheat from the chaff the way Jefferson did, he thought as he drifted to sleep.

The following evening as they sat down to dinner Bill confessed that he had been reading the Bible.

"That's interesting, are you a Christian as well?" Rob asked.

"I suppose I am to a point" Bill acknowledged "only there are some things in mainstream Christianity that don't sit well with me. For example I don't believe in Heaven and Hell or the Devil and I don't believe a just God would give us only one lifetime. For example how is it just for a baby to die after only a few days compared to people who live a long life, even those who do bad things? To me a religious philosophy must be logical."

"So how do you account for it?" Rob asked.

"I believe in reincarnation" Bill continued "and I also believe that Christ taught reincarnation to His Disciples."

"How do you figure that?" Rob looked puzzled.

"I think that Christ's original teaching included the concept of reincarnation. It was removed for political reasons but there are several Bible passages remaining that indicate that it was indeed His teaching."

"Which passages? Rob asked.

"First of all there's John 9:2 where the Disciples ask Christ why this man was born blind, was it his sin or the sin of his parents? Obviously a person can't have sinned before they're born unless they've lived before. Furthermore Matthew 11:14 and 17:10-13 explain that John the Baptist is the reincarnation of Elijah."

"I hadn't thought of it that way" Rob shook his head.

"The other problem I have with Christian ideology" Bill continued "is the doctrine of forgiveness of sins. If Christ died for our sins, why do we bother being good?"

"I think the way it works is that once a person accepts Christ's forgiveness they repent and change their behaviour" Rob explained.

"Well I guess that's OK if they *do* change their behaviour" Bill conceded. "But how can it be fair if a person spends their whole life raping and pillaging and then decides to become a Christian. Shouldn't he pay in some way for those sins?"

Rob was silent.

"The way I see it" Bill continued "is that every person has to pay for their sins. Again I use the example of John 9:2. When the Disciples asked why this man was born blind, was it his sin or the sin of his parents, surely that implies that sins must be paid for."

"But forgiveness is one of the most important lessons of Christianity" Rob protested. "When Christ died on the cross He said "forgive them Father for they know not what they do."

"Yes" Bill agreed "but I think Christ's message is that *we* must learn to forgive. If we don't learn to forgive others it becomes a vicious never ending cycle of hatred and revenge."

Rob nodded "Like in the Middle East and other places rife with religious or ethnic hatred."

"Exactly" Bill agreed. "I think the forgiveness message is more for the benefit of the forgiver rather than the person being forgiven. I agree with you that the Christian message of forgiveness of sins does allow a person to move on and learn to love and so on. That's a good thing if it changes a person's behaviour, but I do think that every person must pay for their sins somewhere along the line."

"Damn, if you're right then I'm in trouble" Rob laughed.

"Me too" Bill grinned. "But at least *I'll* get a chance to make it up in my next lifetime."

That evening Bill settled down again with the Bible only this time he had a pen and paper to record what he thought were Christ's key lessons. His plan was to ignore anything that didn't fit with his own experience and reason. He also theorised that it may be possible to exclude anything that didn't correspond with Christ's overriding golden rule: to love your neighbour as yourself.

His method was to read through the gospels and when he came across a moral principle that made sense to him, he would paraphrase that principle and jot down the chapter and verse references that explained it. The following is the list he came up with:

	Lessons of Christ in Bill's plain language	References
1	Golden rule: Love your neighbour as yourself, even your enemies. Treat others how you would want them to treat you. This incorporates old testament commandments such as: Do not steal Do not murder Do not covet Do not bear false witness Do not commit adultery	Matt. 5:43-47 Matt. 7:12 Matt. 22:37-40 Mark 12:30-31 Luke 6:31-35 Luke 10:25-28 John 5:14 John 8:7 John 13:34 John 15:12 John 15:17
2	Do not judge others. First look at yourself.	Matt. 7:1-5 Mark 4:24 Luke 6:37-42
3	Do not worry about how others see you, it's how God sees you that counts. When you do a good deed or give charity, don't advertise it: keep it to yourself.	Matt. 6:1-4 Matt. 6:19-20
4	The truth is available to those who seek it.	Matt. 7:7 Luke 11:9
5	Life is a series of difficult challenges. Do what's right, not what's easy.	Matt. 7:13-14 Luke 13:24
6	Beware of false prophets that may be wolves in sheep's clothing, you'll know them by their actions (fruits).	Matt. 7:15-16 Matt. 24:11 Matt. 24:24 Mark 13:5-6 Mark 13:21-22 Luke 6:43-45

7	It's what you do that counts, not what you say. Your rewards are in accordance with your actions. Don't say one thing and do another (don't be a hypocrite).	Matt. 7:16-26 Matt. 16:27 Matt.18:20 Matt. 23:3-4 Matt. 23:25-29 Mark 12:38-40 Luke 6:47 Luke 11:39 Luke 12:56-59 Luke 20:45
8	We must have faith. When we have faith we can do anything. When we have faith we don't need to be afraid.	Matt. 8:26 Matt. 14:31 Matt. 17:20 Matt. 21:21-22 Mark 4:40 Luke 12:25-32 Luke 17:6 John 14:27
9	Evil comes from within a person, not from an external "devil."	Matt. 15:11-20 Mark 6:15-23
10	We must learn to forgive others.	Matt. 6:14 Matt. 18:35 Mark 11:26
11	Don't build your life around material possessions, rather build your soul.	Matt. 6:19-20 Matt. 19:23-24 Mark 10:23-25 Luke 12:15-23
12	It's never too late to turn yourself around.	Matt. 19:26 Matt. 20:10-16 Mark 10:27
13	Be humble. We are all equal.	Matt. 18:4 Matt. 23:5-12 John 13-16

14	We never know when the end will come for us so we must be prepared. Live every day like it might be your last.	Matt. 25:1-13 Mark 13:32-37 Luke 12:40
15	Don't be lazy. Do your share.	Matt. 25:15-30
16	We serve God by serving our fellow man.	Matt. 25:35-40 Luke 10:29-37 John 13:14
17	You can't hide your sins. All is known and you will be judged accordingly.	Mark 4:22 John 3:20-21 Luke 12:2-3 Luke 12:58-59
18	We must persevere on the path of righteousness (perfecting our soul). Don't get side-tracked.	Mark 4:4-20 Luke 8:5-17
19	Be charitable and have compassion for your fellow man.	Mark 12:43-44 Luke 10:29-37
20	Our goal is to perfect our soul and Christ is the model of perfection.	Matt. 5:48 Matt. 19:21

When Bill got home from the road trip he showed the list to Sarah. "It's amazing how short the list actually is. I only came up with about 20 principles and some of them even cross over each other" he explained. "It's such a huge book and there are so many massive Church institutions that claim they need to exist just so they can explain it all to us. And yet it can all be condensed into a few simple lessons."

"How do you know you got them all?" Sarah quizzed him.

"Of course I may have missed some, but I reckon I have the vast majority of them."

"Have you looked at the parables?" Sarah asked "Are they in your list?"

"Yes I jotted down the lessons I thought they were telling me" Bill nodded.

"That's good because it's the parables that I remember from my youth" Sarah commented. "The story of the good Samaritan is unforgettable. Maybe that's why there are long-winded stories, because it's the stories we remember."

"You might be onto something there Sarah. The stories also put the lesson in a context so we can understand it better. It doesn't even matter if the stories themselves are true or not. It's the lesson from the stories that's important and the story helps us to remember the lesson. Even the story of Christ's life wasn't written down until at least fifty years after His death, so there are bound to be a few details that weren't accurate. But again, it doesn't matter. What matters are the lessons we learn from the story of His life.

I guess that's what Rob was getting at when he was talking about following the way of Christ. The main thing I got out of all of this is that we need to be good, but the problem is what "being good" actually means. It's through His *example* that we can know what good is."

Sarah smiled "You're really getting into this aren't you."

"Yeah I'm on a bit of a roll" Bill grinned. "Maybe other religions have the same lessons but just different stories. It would be interesting to investigate how many of these lessons are included in other religions. But when am I going to find the time?"

Sarah looked at Bill kindly "That job of yours is really getting you down isn't it. Why don't you toss it in and finish your book. We don't need the money that badly."

"Thanks Sarah, that's exactly what I'll do. I love you."

Chapter 5—The Buddhist

"Everyone thinks of changing the world, but no one thinks of changing himself" Leo Tolstoy

Once Bill had resigned from his job he was free to continue with his research for his book on religion, but initially he found it difficult to make progress. He had already known a lot about Christianity so that part had been quite easy for him. However when it came to the other major religions the task ahead seemed quite daunting. How could he glean the key lessons without years of study into each?

He had the opportunity to talk to Hamish after a Junto meeting and decided to seek his advice. He told him about his progress to date and that he was having difficulty taking the next step. "I just don't know where to start Hamish, it's such a huge task" he grumbled.

Hamish listened patiently and finally responded "There's an old Chinese proverb that says a journey of a thousand miles must begin with a single step. Just make a start and it will come to you. First of all clearly define what you're looking for and then start looking. You'll be surprised how easily it will come. Be on the lookout for the answers because they may come in unexpected ways when you least expect it."

"Seek and you will find" Bill commented.

"Precisely" Hamish smiled. "You'll be astounded to find how true that saying really is. Did you notice how you just happened to meet the right people at the right time when you were investigating Christianity?"

"I guess so" Bill agreed hesitantly.

"You know so!" Hamish exclaimed. "By the way how did you get on with my friend Simon?"

Bill had been so busy since his return from the USA that he had quite forgotten to tell Hamish about his trip. He gave Hamish a full account of his meeting in Washington DC.

Hamish listened intently and gave Bill a pat on the back saying "You've done extremely well Bill."

Bill felt more encouraged after his conversation with Hamish but was still not sure where to start or even which religion to start on. He had a number of books on religions of the world but decided to go to the local library to see what might be available. There were only a small number of books on religion because this was a small town library. Most were on Christianity and he ignored that section. There were only a handful of books on other religions in a separate section. He was quite disappointed as there didn't seem to be anything that wasn't covered in books he already owned.

He was just about to walk away when he glanced down and noticed copies of his own books on the bottom shelf under the Philosophy section. In a moment of vanity, he bent down to pick one of them up and, as he did so, his eyes passed over the Christianity section and he noticed a book that seemed to glare at him with the title *"Jesus and Buddha—the parallel sayings."*

He picked it up and started to read the introduction: ""There is only one truth, not many," say the Buddhist texts. It is open to all. "See and know this for yourself," said the Buddha."

Bill was astonished. This is amazing, has someone already done it for me? Seek and you will find . . . Hamish was right, he thought.

Excitedly he took the book to the library reading room and soon became engrossed. The editor, Marcus Borg, had gone to great lengths in order to match sayings and passages from the Gospels with sayings attributed to Buddha from the numerous texts that comprise Buddhism. Bill thought that some were a bit of a stretch, possibly to fill out the book, but many of the key ones were a perfect match.

He got to a passage comparing Christ's teaching on hypocrisy, reminding us to take the log out of our own eye before trying to take the speck from our neighbour's eye, with a similar statement by Buddha that the faults of others are easier to see than one's own. Bill was chuckling and nodding quietly to himself when a voice interrupted his thoughts.

He looked up and a middle-aged lady was staring across the reading table at him saying something about Jesus. "I'm sorry I was engrossed in my book" Bill replied "What did you say?"

"I said is that book about Jesus?" she repeated.

"Oh, yes it compares the sayings of Jesus with the sayings of Buddha."

"What church do you go to?" she asked out of the blue.

"Ah . . . I don't often go to any church" he replied. "Occasionally I go to the Anglican Church."

"How can you stand them?" the lady snapped.

"What do you mean?" Bill asked timidly.

"Well I used to go there but now they're so liberal, I mean they're allowing homosexuals to be ministers and I don't think that's right."

"Oh, I don't know much about that" Bill responded. "What church do you go to now?"

"I went to the Baptist Church for a while but the minister there was a total idiot. I go to an out of town church now, Assembly of God."

"Oh" Bill nodded, and looked back down at his book hoping this would disengage the conversation.

The tactic didn't work however and the lady proceeded to tell him how the girls in the library didn't do their job properly, that they didn't put the magazines in the right places. Next it was one of the local shopkeepers who came in for criticism, followed by a string of others with whom she worked.

Bill breathed a sigh of relief when she finally said "Well my lunch break's over. See you another time."

"Yes, nice talking to you" Bill smiled as she walked out.

I guess there's a lesson for me here Bill thought to himself. It doesn't matter which church you attend, it's the way you think and act that counts.

When he got home he found Sarah, reading her emails. She smiled as he came in. "Did you find what you wanted at the library?"

"Yes I found this amazing book" he announced, holding it up for her to see.

"That's great, so you're in a good mood."

"Yes, is there something you want?" he joked.

Sarah looked up from the computer "Well, since you asked . . . you know how we never got to go to Ayres Rock when we travelled around Australia?"

"Ah huh."

"Well there's a special on flights to Ayres Rock right now. Can we afford it?"

Bill grinned "Of course darling." He knew how much Sarah had wanted to go and climb Ayres Rock, which was now more politically correctly named "Uluru." Bill had heard too that the Government was thinking of closing the rock for climbing to satisfy the demands of aboriginal people who claimed the rock was sacred and that climbing it was disrespectful to their culture.

Within a few days they were flying over Lake Eyre, which was full of water for the third year in a row, despite previous dire predictions from climate change alarmists that this would never happen again. It was a beautiful sight, channels through the hot arid desert from all directions flowed into this great inland sea.

Bill and Sarah were excited as they approached for landing. They could see the great Australian icon through the window and it looked exactly like all the picture postcards and tourist brochures. They disembarked at the airport amidst dozens of tourists from all around the world to be shuttled to the resort. There was hardly an Australian accent between them. Bill was surprised that there were virtually no Aboriginal people amongst the tourist operators. "I thought they owned this place" Bill remarked to Sarah. "You'd think they would be working here in great numbers."

They booked their shuttle bus to the rock for the following morning. When Bill asked about climbing the rock he was greeted with frowns from the tourist operators. "Climbing the rock is dangerous and not encouraged" the receptionist warned. "There have been thirty-five people killed in the process of climbing the rock over the years. Most people just walk *around* the rock. It's a beautiful ten kilometre walk."

The brochures about the rock were similarly discouraging in regard to climbing. "We didn't come all this way just to stand there looking at it" Sarah said sternly as soon as they were out of earshot of the reception. Bill nodded but said nothing.

The next morning they were up very early to be taken to the sunrise viewing area. They waited with dozens of other chattering tourists with their cameras to see the first of the sun's rays alighting on the rock. Bill thought it was all quite fun but a little overrated.

"I can't wait to climb it" Sarah said as they got back on the bus that was to take them to the base of the rock. The bus driver was friendly and more helpful in regard to climbing. "They close the rock for climbing when the wind gets up" he explained. "There's a sign at the bottom that tells you whether it's open or not. If you want to climb it you'd better get cracking because the wind is starting to get up and they *will* close it."

They read the sign that said something about possible fifteen thousand dollar fines for anyone trying to climb the rock when the closed sign was up. More importantly though the sign said that it was currently open. A small group of people were already on their way up. The first part of the ascent was very steep but thankfully there was a chain attached to the rock that climbers could cling to. Bill found the going very tough partly because he wasn't as fit as he used to be, but also because he was tall and the chain was either built for midgets or perhaps better suited for people to crawl on their hands and knees. It did suit some of the young Japanese tourists however who almost ran past Bill and Sarah.

Fear of heights was something that had plagued Bill over the years but he had learned to control it to an extent by avoiding looking down and rationalising his position. Today he repeatedly told himself there is a chain, it's OK I can't fall as long as I don't have a heart attack or something. Sarah was in front and despite also having a fear of heights she seemed to be doing quite well. She was moving quickly to keep up with a young American man by the name of Andy they had been chatting to earlier. Bill found himself short of breath and struggled to keep up.

What made matters worse was the wind that had seemed only gentle on the ground, was now roaring fiercely. So much so, that between the noise of Bill's shirt flapping and the roar of the wind itself Bill couldn't make himself heard as he shouted to Sarah who was only a few metres in front.

They were now about two thirds of the way up the steep face of the rock. Bill could no longer stand. He sat down, clinging grimly to the chain. He looked down and saw that there was no longer anyone behind him. People were starting to return from above him. They must have closed the rock he thought. He looked up towards the top of the rock where the chain ran out. A young man shimmied around him on the chain and said he had been to the top of the chain but it was too dangerous to go further. The wind was simply too strong.

He knew now that they had to go back. He shouted at the top of his voice to Sarah. She was only about ten meters in front of him but it was no use. His voice was carried away uselessly by the howling wind. She was still striving to catch up with Andy who had now moved ahead somewhat. Finally she turned around to see Bill sitting motionless, clutching the chain. "Come on!" she yelled "We can make it!" Although Bill couldn't hear her words he could read her lips and her beckoning motions, but he wasn't going anywhere.

She shimmied back down the chain to him and shouted again that they could still make it perhaps after a rest. Bill shook his head. "There's no point in going on" he screamed "Look up there where the chain run's out. If there was no chain to hang onto we'd be blown off the rock!"

She sat down beside him. "We've come all this way we *have* to get to the top. I'll go on without you" she threatened. "I'll catch up with Andy."

"No way!" Bill bellowed. "I'm not going to let you kill yourself! We *have* to go back down!"

They had reached a stalemate. They both sat for several minutes in silence. Finally Sarah conceded. They started to descend. When they reached the bottom they saw that the sign was indeed up saying the rock was closed to climbing.

Sarah had now become very despondent. Bill on the other hand was just glad to be down safely. He tried to cheer Sarah up. "We can still walk around it" he said "and we can come back tomorrow and try again."

"You heard the weather report" Sarah grumbled. "The wind is going to be worse tomorrow, that was the only chance we had. You brought me all this way out here and you were too much of a wimp to climb it" she added as they sat in some shade. To add to Bill's anguish Andy then came trotting up saying he had made it to the top. "You see we were nearly there" Sarah sneered.

Bill knew how disappointed Sarah was but there was nothing he could do about it. He tried to be positive about the walk around the rock. "We can still make it around the rock and get back in time for our shuttle bus pickup time if we don't dawdle" he beckoned. As they walked Sarah started to cheer up slightly though she lagged behind Bill taking numerous photos. When they got about three quarters of the way around Bill realised they wouldn't make it back in time for the bus unless they really hurried. It wouldn't be the end of the world if they missed it, but the idea of spending several hours waiting for the next bus in the hot sun did not appeal. So they virtually ran the last three kilometres. As they approached Bill could see their bus already loading up passengers. Bill ran on ahead of Sarah to ask the driver to wait. "No worries mate" the driver grinned.

As Bill waited he looked across at the sign. It said: "OPEN."

"Look Sarah we can have another go" Bill declared as Sarah arrived gasping for breath.

"You bastard" Sarah sobbed, sweat and tears streaming down her face. "You made me run all that way and now you want me to climb up there!"

"We can do it" Bill grinned.

When Sarah had finally stopped puffing she put her hands on her hips smiled and said "OK let's do it."

Again it was tough going and still windy when they got to the same point they had previously reached, but this time quite tolerable. When they got past the end of the chain the trail was marked with stripes of white paint. The route was now up hill and down dale and it wasn't possible to see where you were on the rock. They had gone about ten minutes past the top of the chain when they met several people on their way down. "Are we far from the top now?" Bill asked.

An exhausted looking young woman smiled and said "I'm afraid you're only about a quarter of the way."

When she was out of earshot Sarah let fly. "That bitch, if she's telling the truth I don't want to know about it. Why couldn't she say something positive like you're almost there or something?"

"Maybe she was kidding" Bill suggested hopefully.

It turned out that the young woman wasn't joking at all. It was an awful long way to the top. However the going was undulating. It was more across than it was up. They started to enjoy the adventure and to forget about their aches and pains. After about half an hour Bill said "Hey Sarah, that Andy guy, he was lying. He could never have made it to the top."

Sarah nodded "Yeah he must have just got to the top of the chain and thought that was it."

They laughed together and continued now with a new lease of life stemming from a mutual sense of purpose. In places the going was very scary. They reached one particular place that was very steep and a slip could mean a fall of hundreds of metres and certain death. Sarah grimly made the traverse but Bill held back reluctant as he didn't trust the boots he was wearing. "Now I wish I packed those hiking boots" he yelled to Sarah who was now safely across the dangerous zone. As he sat contemplating his imminent possible death, knowing that he would *have* to do it eventually another group returned from the top. They took an alternate route that was steep but the consequence of slipping was more likely a broken leg than certain death. Bill thanked God as he took this alternate route.

When they finally reached the top they were euphoric. "We made it" Bill cried, they hugged and kissed. There was another couple at the top enjoying the view who offered to take their photo.

"I suddenly feel old" Bill sighed as he looked down at the two grinning six year old children who were also there with their Mum and Dad.

The way down was tough going too as their aging and aching joints felt all the jolts. But it didn't matter, they were in heaven, they had been to the top. They slumped onto the seats near the car park in the welcome shade and enjoyed some lukewarm water that tasted like nectar.

"The trouble is now we have to wait for the next shuttle" Bill declared.

"I don't mind" Sarah responded. "We've done what we came to do."

They slouched back on the seats and Bill was almost nodding off to sleep when a voice startled him.

"Are you waiting for the shuttle bus?"

Bill looked up and was surprised to see a man of South East Asian appearance in a bright orange robe standing in front of them. "Oh hi, yes but we have some time to wait I think" he replied, rubbing his eyes to make sure he wasn't dreaming. "Are you waiting too?"

"Yes I am."

"Are you a Buddhist monk by any chance?" Bill asked hesitantly.

"Yes how can you tell?" the monk grinned.

"Oh you know. I was guessing from your clothing. But that's quite amazing that we should meet you out here."

"Why is that?"

"Well I didn't think you guys travelled much" Bill replied. But there was a more profound reason why Bill thought this encounter to be amazing. He had just been ruminating over the Buddhism section in his book and suddenly a Buddhist monk appeared, as large as life, right here in this unexpected place.

The monk laughed "Do you think we spend our whole lives shut away in a monastery?"

"Oh no, I didn't mean to be rude" Bill stammered. "Where are you from?"

"I'm from Thailand. I'm here as a tourist also. See, here is my camera." He held his camera up jokingly. "Actually I'm in Australia to lecture but I'm lucky enough to get some time to do some sightseeing. You two look exhausted" he remarked.

"Yeah we've had a tough day. We climbed the rock" Sarah sighed. "It was great though. Have you climbed the rock?" she asked.

"Oh no, I don't think my shoes would be suitable" the monk laughed pointing to his sandals.

Bill smiled "My name is Bill and this is my wife Sarah."

"My name is Mano, pleased to meet you" the quite elderly monk replied as he sat on an adjacent seat.

"Actually" Bill continued "it's uncanny that we should meet you here because I'm researching for a book and I need some advice about Buddhism. Will you help me please?"

"Certainly, I'll do my best. What would you like to know?"

"Well I've been studying the similarities between Christianity and Buddhism."

Mano nodded thoughtfully "Yes, I understand there has been a somewhat parallel path between Buddhism in the East and Christianity in the West. Christianity emerged from Judaism through a great teacher in a similar way to how Buddhism was established from Hinduism via our great teacher."

"Yes that's true" Bill agreed "but I'm particularly interested in the teachings themselves." Bill reached into his pocket and unfolded a piece of paper that had a typed list of the twenty "lessons of Christ" that he had drawn up from his reading of the Gospels. "These are my own interpretations of the teachings of Christ" he stated. "Would you mind casting your eyes over them and telling me which of them you consider would also be applicable to the teachings of Buddha please?"

Mano took several minutes to read and reflect on the page before finally lifting his head. "These are also the teachings of the Buddha" he said.

Bill was astonished. "What, all of them?"

"Yes I believe so" Mano nodded.

"Wow!" Bill exclaimed "I wonder how come that is. Do you think it's possible that Jesus learned Buddhism while growing up or perhaps Christian teaching has crept into Buddhist writings?"

Mano shook his head "I suppose you can't rule out either of those possibilities, but I prefer to believe that they both taught us the lessons independently of one another. The Truth is the Truth; it's not the possession of any one teacher. The lessons are universal and may be discovered by all genuine seekers."

"Yes I've heard that before" Bill agreed. "Did you notice if there's anything missing from the list that Buddhism teaches?"

Mano cast his eyes over the list again "Well, there is one small thing I notice. It's about the company we keep. The Buddha teaches us to be careful who we associate with. That if we associate with fools and bad people we may become like them. He says that if you can't find good and virtuous people to associate with then it is better not to associate with anyone."

"Is that why you guys tend to live in monasteries to keep away from all of us fools?" Bill asked cheekily.

Mano laughed "Do you think we are a bunch of snobs?"

"No" Bill responded awkwardly "But, from a Christian viewpoint, Christ was known to associate with lowly people."

"Perhaps Bill, but the people who chose to follow Christ were not fools; they knew they were on the right path. But there is a good reason for this teaching about associations. It's because of something we call peer pressure. We tend to adopt the thinking and behaviour of the group we belong to. So if we're in a bad group we may become bad also."

"I can see what you're saying" Bill acknowledged. "It's a very pertinent point with teenagers especially. I have a nephew who got into bad company and it had a really negative effect on him. With young people too, they are often misled when they fall for a member of the opposite sex with corrupt ideas."

"Blinded by love" Sarah interjected.

"Exactly" Mano agreed "Teenagers are very susceptible, especially if they don't have good grounding in right thinking and a moral code to live by, but it's not just teenagers. It happens to us all. We are all influenced by the company we keep. The culture or religion we belong to has an especially profound influence on our thinking."

"You're spot on there" Bill concurred. "You could attribute most of the world's problems to the "group think" phenomenon. "OK, you've convinced me to choose my peer group carefully. What else does Buddhism teach that is absent in Christianity? For one thing what's with all the meditating?"

"So you think we spend all day long sitting around meditating" Mano chuckled. "Contrary to popular opinion we actually do a lot of work. The monasteries don't run themselves you know and there's a lot of learning and teaching to do. But seriously though, I'm not a specialist in meditation. In my country we have two separate kinds of monks. One kind specialises in meditation and the other specialises in scholarly teachings, study and so on. I am from the scholarly school.

Nevertheless, meditation is an important part of Buddhism, as you say, but I think it's often misunderstood. Some people, particularly in the West, think that sitting around chanting a mantra is all it takes to achieve enlightenment. This is far from the truth. The primary purpose of meditation is to calm your mind, so you become "mindful" of your desires. Once you have calmed your mind you can control it. Disciplining our minds is the key. Most of our problems stem from a lack of self-discipline. When we learn to discipline our mind we can also discipline our actions."

"Maybe I should try meditation" Bill commented. "Self-discipline is definitely a problem for me. I want to study but it's so much easier to sit around watching television. I guess you guys don't have television."

"There are indeed fewer temptations in the monastery" Mano grinned. "But actually we do have access to a television. We're not totally deprived you know. One of the Buddha's key messages is to take the "middle" way between self-indulgence and austerity."

"You mean moderation" Bill suggested. "That sounds sensible. But when the temptation is there how do you avoid excess?"

"It's not easy, but few worthwhile things in life are easy. Changing our behaviour is usually about changing our habits. We must substitute good habits for bad habits. Once we've decided to adopt a new habit we need to say to ourselves when the old thinking habits start to kick in: "I don't do that anymore" or "I don't think like that anymore."

The main thing to realise is that it all comes down to the choices we make. We are free to choose self-control over self-indulgence, reason over passion, tolerance over hatred and so on. And we must inevitably suffer the consequences or reap the benefits of the thoughts we choose."

"So" Bill interrupted, "are you suggesting that everything that happens to us originates from the thoughts that we choose?"

"Yes, all that we experience stems from the thoughts that we choose in our own minds. All action originates in thought. Bad thoughts lead to bad actions which in turn lead to our suffering. Pure thoughts lead to good actions that lead us away from suffering. Evil or hateful thoughts can never lead to good results, even though there may sometimes be a temporary advantage. In the long run the evil doer will pay for his actions."

"You mean through karma" Bill offered.

"Yes" Mano replied. "Are you familiar with the concept of karma?"

"Oh yes absolutely and I believe in it. It seems a most reasonable philosophy. And it goes hand in hand with the idea of reincarnation. What are your views on reincarnation?"

"Well this is a complicated area in which you might get different answers, depending on which sect of Buddhism you ask. Buddhism has many variants, just like other religions."

"Do you mean you have dogmas depending on which sect you come from?" Bill asked.

"Well you could say that" Mano responded "but we prefer to think we don't have dogmas as such. Even though there are various philosophies, we are not obliged to accept any particular viewpoint if it doesn't make sense to us. We are encouraged to keep questioning until we are satisfied with the answer. We are more concerned with the discipline than the theology, so to speak."

"So I guess you don't burn heretics at the stake" Bill quipped.

Mano laughed "No but to be fair, like all religions we do have many sects, each of which has their own rituals and beliefs. Many of these have arisen through mixing the Buddhist teaching with other religious practices or cultural beliefs particular to a region."

"The same thing has arisen in Christianity" Bill remarked.

"Of course it's inevitable" Mano replied. "It has advantages and disadvantages. It's easier for people to accept the new teaching if some of their old religion is incorporated. On the other hand we have to accept the superstition and mumbo-jumbo that gets carried forward into the new faith."

"Yeah tell me about it" Bill nodded. "So getting back to reincarnation do you believe, like the Hindus, that people can come back as animals?"

Mano shook his head "No, this idea makes no sense to me. As I said, Buddhism teaches that man has free will to choose his thoughts and actions. He can decide to choose right or wrong action. The wise person will choose right over evil. Obviously animals cannot do this, they have no volition. If a person came back as an animal they could not resolve their karma."

"I'm glad to hear you say that" Bill responded. "Because I've heard the Dalai Lama talking about "sentient beings" implying that humans and animals are no different and statements like "even an insect can become the Buddha."

Mano raised his hands defensively "Well as I said there are many different schools of thought in Buddhism. Even the meaning of the term sentient beings is widely debated by scholars. The Dalai Lama is of course a Tibetan Buddhist from the Mahayana school of Buddhism. This is significantly different from my own more traditional school called Theravada. Animism is certainly part of Tibetan Buddhism, but you will also find it in some areas in my country too, where animism was part of the traditional religions."

"Thanks for clearing that up" Bill acknowledged. "Because it concerns me that the animism coming from some parts of Buddhism is giving strength to a rather ugly phenomenon developing in the West: the atheistic environmental religion that allows animals to be put ahead of people."

Mano nodded "I know what you mean, but the sentimentality towards animals is understandable. We observe the suffering of animals and we feel empathy towards them. It is indeed a virtue to be compassionate, but at the end of the day there is little we can do about the suffering of animals, or even people for that matter. The only person we can really change is our self and ultimately therefore we can only prevent our own suffering."

"What about when we give to others that are less fortunate than ourselves?" Bill asked. "I mean that must help alleviate their suffering somewhat?"

"That's a popular idea Bill and of course charity may sometimes be a virtue, but it's not as simple as you might think. Charity often does more harm than good in the long run. Each person is in the circumstances they are in for a reason. They may have karma to resolve or they may be learning a particular lesson or perhaps they are in certain circumstances to teach others. Whatever the case, our interference in their life's journey may not be warranted. It takes a wise person to discern what can be done for others that will not harm them. Most charity actually stems from a feeling of guilt. So the "giving" is done more to appease one's own sense of guilt and is therefore basically done out of self-interest.

Ultimately we are all responsible for ourselves and must accept that responsibility. There is nothing inherently unjust or unfair in the world that requires us to go around trying to put the world to rights. There are people who think they are doing "good" by trying to address injustices they perceive in the world."

"We call them do-gooders" Bill nodded.

"Yes" Mano continued "but this mistaken attitude will more likely do harm, not only to the person they are helping but also to themselves. The universal law of karma is perfect. We live in the world that we deserve to live in. The circumstances we find ourselves in inevitably make us face the problems we need to solve in order to address the flaws we have in our character. If we don't resolve those deficiencies we will continually find ourselves in similar circumstances until we do resolve them."

"I think I've experienced that" Bill interjected. "For example I was sent to a boarding school where there were mostly rich kids. My family wasn't rich and I think I needed to learn humility and to avoid jealousy and bitterness. I don't think I resolved it then because when I left school I was more jealous and bitter than ever but I have throughout my life often encountered similar circumstances."

"And he's still got no humility" Sarah joked.

"Yeah I keep bashing my head up against the same old wall" Bill chuckled.

Mano laughed "Of course if you realise that you have a shortfall in your character you're half way there. Even when you think you've addressed it though, you need to be careful not to regress into the old habits of thinking, it's easy to do. We need to be vigilant."

"Yeah, still a way to go there . . ." Bill said. "By the way, for those rich kids, is it a curse to be rich?"

Mano shook his head slowly "Wealth is not necessarily a problem in the hands of the wise person if used for good. It is the craving for wealth that is the biggest problem."

"I can understand that" Bill nodded. "Getting back to helping others, if we can't generally interfere in the lives of others to help them, what can we do?"

"We can teach, we can help others to uplift themselves but only if they are ready and they want your help. Above all we can be an example to others by living the Dharma."

"What is the Dharma?" Bill asked.

"It is living your life according to the principles explained by the Buddha" Mano responded. "To give up inappropriate desire through self-control, to give up selfish thoughts such as hatred, jealousy, vanity, anger, gluttony, and so on, to be considerate of those around you, to reject violence and to seek wisdom."

"What do you mean by wisdom?" Bill interrupted.

"Wisdom is to know the right choices for any given circumstance and to make those right choices accordingly."

Bill nodded "I guess then the big question is to figure out what the right choices are. Does that mean that much of our life is about figuring out what's right and what's wrong?"

"Absolutely" Mano agreed. "But it's our actions that really count. We can discern what the right path is from the teachings of the great ones. But, unless we act accordingly, the knowledge in itself is useless."

"That makes sense" Bill agreed. "So once we've figured out right from wrong and act accordingly, what happens then?"

Mano thought for a few moments before replying "once you have achieved ultimate wisdom, live a virtuous life, have got rid of your cravings and selfishness through self-control and have resolved all karma, then you might say you have achieved nirvana which means you no longer need to be reborn."

"Is that like becoming perfect?" Bill asked.

"Yes, I believe so, or at least as perfect as it is possible for us to become. I think of it as becoming like the Buddha who is the enlightened one."

"Or, perhaps in Christian terms, to be a saint or living the example of Christ" Sarah suggested quietly.

At that point the shuttle bus pulled up. Bill thanked Mano very much for sharing his great insights with them.

That evening Bill and Sarah celebrated their success in climbing the rock with dinner at one of the resort restaurants. Their waitress, to Bill's surprise, was a young aboriginal girl. Bill took the opportunity to ask her why there weren't more aboriginal people working at the resort.

"It's a sad state of affairs I'm afraid" the young girl replied. "There are very few from my home Mutitjulu community who work here or work anywhere for that matter. The community is rife with drug and alcohol abuse and even child abuse. Although I come from there I'm not really part of the community anymore. I was lucky enough to get a scholarship to go to a boarding school in Adelaide. I just come back here for the holidays and work in the resort."

"Do you see your friends and family when you come back though?" Sarah asked.

"To be honest no, not really" the young girl replied. "I do visit my mum but I avoid contact with my old friends. We're different now. They are all into drugs and alcohol and some of them even sniff petrol. I count myself lucky. If I was still there I might be the same."

"What about when you finish school, will you come back then?" Sarah enquired.

"I'll probably go to Uni. After that I don't know. There's nothing here for me so I can't really see myself coming back. I would love to do something that would change the culture in my community but honestly I don't think anyone can. The only way I've been able to change myself is through getting away from that environment and living amongst other people. I think the only thing I can do is to make something of myself and try to be an example to other young aboriginal people."

"Is there no hope for your community then?" Bill asked.

"Well the Government has tried all sorts of things to intervene but the problems remain. They don't trust outsiders anyway."

"Perhaps they would trust you" Sarah suggested "if you were to go back later when you've finished your studies."

"Maybe, I have my doubts" the girl replied. "What can I get you for dessert?"

Bill and Sarah spent much of the following day lounging around the swimming pool at the resort. They were glad to be able to relax after the exertion of the day before. At the poolside they started talking to a middle-aged couple with English cockney accents who apparently ran a business providing "spiritual journeys" in the "sacred geography" of the outback for new age "seekers".

The woman said she was a spirit medium and when they weren't running these tours she claimed to do past life regressions, divination and spiritual healing. Bill shuddered as she raved about the teachings of a certain archangel whom she "channelled" and who apparently provided her with guidance.

Thankfully they did not stay long at the pool and as soon as they had departed Bill sighed "thank goodness they've gone."

"I know you hate that new age stuff" Sarah sympathised.

"Yes, but it's interesting you know. I've been studying primitive religions with their shamanism, witchcraft and so on and the new age mumbo jumbo is actually pretty similar. I think that both primitive and new age religions embrace all the worst aspects of religion without the good things. I mean they're dominated by superstition, dogma and rituals. The lessons about noble behaviour, virtuous living, loving your neighbour and so on are absent. It's a bit like what Mano was saying about some people's approach to meditation. Seekers are offered an easy way to enlightenment or salvation by doing a few rituals without doing the hard work."

"But don't priests in other religions do that too?" Sarah queried.

"Good point" Bill laughed. "I guess they've all learned they need to keep the rituals and dogma going to maintain their powerful positions within the tribe or congregation or whatever."

Chapter 6—The Philosopher

"A little philosophy inclineth man's mind to atheism, but depth in philosophy bringeth men's minds about to religion" Francis Bacon

After returning from Ayres Rock Bill needed to visit his University to sort out some details regarding the deferment of his PhD, which he had put on hold. While he was there he noticed an advertisement for a lecture on ethics to be delivered by a certain "world famous philosopher" by the name of Professor Clive Drek to be hosted by the University's Philosophy Department that very evening. Bill had seen the man's face on television before but had never actually listened to what he had to say and decided to stay for the lecture. Given the man's credentials he thought it would certainly be an interesting presentation.

Professor Drek was introduced as "the world's leading ethicist" having won numerous awards from various universities. He began by giving some background about himself, explaining that his grandparents had been murdered in a concentration camp by the Nazis and that this was one of the main motivations for him becoming an ethicist. He wanted to ensure that the horror of the holocaust never happened again. He explained that he was driven by a sense of moral justice. This all sounded very noble and whetted Bill's appetite for what he thought would be an interesting presentation. However his eager anticipation was short-lived.

Drek had gone on to say that he was an atheist. He claimed that if God existed He would not have allowed the holocaust to happen. In any case the existence of God had been well and truly disproven by science beyond any doubt. He pointed out that human beings were merely animals who had come to dominate the other species on the planet by chance and that Darwin had proved this. His argument then went on to say that if humans were merely animals then they should not be given any more respect than other animals, claiming that it was morally wrong to treat animals as lesser creatures. "Surely an able-bodied ape has more value than a disabled human" he said emotionlessly.

Bill's skin started to crawl when further into the talk the quietly spoken professor insisted that it was morally okay to kill people who wouldn't be likely to have a good quality of life, for example disabled newborn babies or old people who were no longer valuable. He cited the case of his own mother who had suffered Alzheimer's disease and if he'd had his way she would have been euthanized.

The lecture then went on to a long rambling discussion on how humans were destroying the planet and depriving other species through their greed and selfishness. In particular he attacked those who didn't accept the idea that humans were causing dangerous climate change through their carbon dioxide emissions, likening them to holocaust deniers.

Bill breathed a sigh of relief when the lecture finally came to an end. He had thought of leaving in protest several times but had instead sat in stunned fascination at the bizarre stream of arguments.

At question time a young student asked whether it was okay to have sex with animals. The audience laughed when Drek replied that it would be fine as long the animal was enjoying it and wasn't being exploited.

By now Bill was churning up inside. He wondered how a man with such a warped sense of morality could be held in such high esteem. He was thinking of standing up and giving this so-called professor a piece of his mind but hesitated because it seemed the entire audience had lapped it up, judging from the rapturous applause. He was musing on that thought when another man stood up to ask a question.

He introduced himself as Graham, a lecturer in philosophy at the University. "Given what you said about the morality of the Nazis, how can you justify your position on euthanasia, which seems to me quite similar to the Nazi ideas on eugenics?"

Oh boy, yes what an irony Bill thought. How's he going to respond to that?

But he never got a chance. Graham had been accosted by a group of students wearing animal rights T-shirts. They started to abuse him and were physically pushing him around. Thankfully there were two security guards in the room who came over and escorted the offending students out.

The organiser then quickly wound up the lecture and Drek left. Bill was left scratching his head. As he went out he could see that there was still an altercation going on in the corridor between Graham and a group of students who were jeering at him. Graham finally lost his cool and yelled "get lost" in such a loud voice that it seemed to startle the students and they left.

Bill caught up to Graham as he headed down the corridor. "Excuse me I heard what you said in there and I think it was very brave of you in front of that hostile crowd."

"Thanks I appreciate that" the man smiled warmly.

"No problem, my name is Bill. Actually I wonder if you could help me please. You see I'm researching for a book on religion at the moment and I'd be interested to hear your views on religion from a philosophical point of view. I had hoped I might get something useful from Drek's lecture, but all I got was that his atheism and green politics are about as fanatical as any religious fundamentalist I've ever met."

"I thought so to" Graham grinned. "I'd love to help. Would you like to join me in the cafeteria for a coffee?"

As they sat down with their coffee Graham continued "What you said about Drek being a fanatic, I agree and a dangerous one at that. I think he is actually worse than a religious fanatic because his morals are warped. Because he has no God he has no boundaries and therefore he can use his cold hearted so-called logic to justify almost anything. His logic is the same as that used by the Nazi's to justify their atrocities."

"Yes, I liked the way you pointed that out to the audience" Bill complimented.

"Thanks, but as I expected, it didn't go down well" Graham laughed. "The most frightening things about him are his popularity and his position. Whenever the Government or the media want some input on ethics or morals he's the one they go to. They go to people like him because they're scared to ask religious folks because religion is no longer politically correct."

"They don't see that he's really a wolf in sheep's clothing" Bill suggested.

"Exactly" Graham agreed. "I'm really concerned that his ideas and those of his kind have infiltrated the public education system in such a big way. School children are being indoctrinated with that kind of nonsense and taught it as Truth."

"Tell me about it" Bill agreed. "How do you reckon he got so popular?"

"He feeds on people's guilt" Graham responded "Especially the young and gullible. He tells them that our evil and greedy generation has destroyed the planet, used up all the resources and so on. Because the kids have been turned off religion he offers them a sense that they are on the moral high ground."

Bill shuddered "save the planet, animal rights, it's all part of the new green religion."

"Yeah, it is a religion" Graham agreed, "But what's more scary is that it's also a political force. Drek even stood in a national election for the Green party. Thankfully he didn't get in but there are plenty more like him. Of course they are still a minority, but they would like to shut the rest of us up. They don't believe in democracy unless we agree with them. They would like to shut down free speech, ban us from eating meat and stop us from using cars. A Green government would be a totalitarian one."

"Politics and religion shouldn't be mixed unless it's the green religion" Bill joked.

"Yes but it's really no joke, it's the truth" Graham responded.

They sat in silence for a few moments before Bill asked "I gather then that you're a bit different to rest of the people in the philosophy department here?"

Graham smiled "I'm not only different to those in my department but almost unique in the philosophy profession these days, in that I'm a Christian."

"Were you always a Christian?"

"Well I was brought up a churchgoing Anglican but when I went to University and studied philosophy I became convinced of the logic of atheism. When I look back on it I think it was easy for the lecturers to convert me and others to atheism. They had a captive audience and we were all too worried about our grades to resist."

"But you're not like that now, what changed you?"

"There are a number of reasons, but I have to admit that it started with a girl I met, a girl that became my wife."

"They can have a lot of influence" Bill chuckled.

"Yeah, but for me I don't think it was blind infatuation. When I started to go out with her I would hang around with some of her friends from church. I noticed what nice people they were. I couldn't help thinking how much nicer they were than my atheist friends. They looked out for each other, contributed to the community and were even quite tolerant of my atheism. Whereas my atheist friends on the other hand were completely intolerant of religion and spent most of their time trying to show others how cool they were. It was all an ego trip for them. So I ended up going back to Christianity."

"What about the dogmas and rituals, how do you find them?" Bill enquired.

"To be honest I don't accept *all* the dogma. For example I don't believe in hell. The idea of eternal damnation doesn't seem consistent with a loving God."

Bill nodded "You don't mind a bit of heresy then?"

Graham laughed "No, I think it's better than intellectual dishonesty. But to me such things are minor considerations. When you look at the overall package of Christianity and compare it with the empty, Godless and loveless philosophy presented by my friends and colleagues from the university there was no contest."

"How was it at work when you went back to Christianity?" Bill asked.

"It was quite difficult actually. I didn't mind it though because I enjoy being a rebel against the group think. But you saw the attitude in that lecture theatre. Basically I've been struggling with that sort of thing for the last twenty years. They tolerate me to my face but I know that they mock me behind my back. Actually I believe there's a prevailing atmosphere within the philosophy profession. It's a kind of smug, self-righteous air of superiority that sneers at the whole idea of religion. It's like "I'm too sophisticated to believe in God.""

95

"I know exactly what you mean Graham and I think it goes way beyond just your philosophy department. It extends to a whole class of people that includes most academics, virtually everyone in the arts community and nearly all journalists. They love to scoff at the deluded uneducated peasants that are so primitive as to believe in God, like it's the same thing as believing in the tooth fairy."

Graham nodded "The post-modern, left-wing, relativist intellectuals. Socrates would have despised them, as he did the "sophists" of his day."

"Tell me about Socrates Graham. For example I've heard about the Socratic method of teaching, what does that mean?"

"Sure, basically Socrates would ask a person a series of questions that would make them have to explain or justify their understanding about a particular topic. He would then point out any inconsistencies in the logic or facts stated by the person. In theory then the person would see the flaws in their thinking which may cause them to change their mind."

"I'm glad you said in theory" Bill remarked. "Try getting a believer in man-made global warming to see the flaws in their logic."

Graham laughed "The point is that Socrates said he wasn't actually imparting any wisdom per se. He argued that he knew nothing about anything but would merely ask questions."

"So his method was to root out the truth by exposing contradictions and falsehoods in a person's thinking" Bill suggested.

"Exactly" Graham continued. "He also found from his questioning that many people thought they were wise, but from the answers they gave to his questions, it was obvious that they weren't wise at all. He figured he was better off than them because at least he *knew* he wasn't wise. Those who thought they were wise could never actually become wise because they were already self-satisfied."

"I guess that's a trap we all fall into" Bill commented. "We become narrow minded and entrenched in our own little world. Just because we might know something about a small aspect of life doesn't mean we know about the whole of life. We don't think outside our paradigm. We may even shut out the obvious truth if it doesn't fit in with our view of the world."

"Dead right" Graham concurred. "And that's the main thing Socrates was on about, that we must always seek the Truth and follow the Truth wherever it leads us."

"I've heard that expression before" Bill interrupted, "But I thought John Locke said it."

"I'm sure they both said it Bill. Actually, although we know it as the words of Socrates, it was Plato who wrote it down. Socrates wrote down nothing and, for all we know, many of the wonderful words attributed to Socrates may have been Plato's. But does it really matter who said it or who said it first? What really matters are the ideas themselves. They're still as relevant today as they were to the philosophers of the enlightenment and to the ancient Greeks two and a half thousand years ago."

"Whew, that's a long time ago" Bill remarked. "Do you reckon Plato's other ideas are still as relevant today?"

"The beauty of philosophy Bill is that the same big philosophical questions are as unanswered today as they were in Plato's day. In fact, I'm ashamed to say that, thanks to the narrow mindedness of modern philosophy, we are probably *less* able to answer them than in Plato's time."

Bill nodded "I must admit I have trouble trying to fathom what modern philosophers are on about. Their texts are so full of jargon and complicated long winded arguments that I wonder if they're just trying to cover up their own confusion. Perhaps they're scared that if the average person could understand them, we'd be able to see that they actually know stuff all about anything."

"Obfuscation" Graham laughed "Yep, I think there's a lot of it about."

"So why haven't we made any progress do you reckon?" Bill asked.

"Well I think one of the main reasons is the restriction of free speech down through the ages. Socrates argued that truth could only come out where people are allowed to speak their ideas freely and those ideas can then be questioned, using his Socratic method."

"So the amount of Truth prevailing in any given society might depend on the level of free speech that's allowed in that society" Bill suggested.

"Yes I think so" Graham agreed. "And free speech has been rare throughout history. Socrates himself was executed for his words and successive religious and authoritarian regimes have muzzled free speech ever since, because it's a threat to their power. It wasn't until after the freethinkers of the enlightenment such as Francis Bacon and John Locke that we had anything like free speech."

"I guess we're lucky to be living in an age and a country that allows free speech" Bill commented.

"Yes but it's something we have to keep fighting for. There are always dark forces that would take away our right to free speech if you give them half a chance. You saw those goons in that lecture theatre. They wanted to shut me up."

"I know what you mean Graham. Actually I think we have a problem with free speech right now because of political correctness. In our multicultural society we're not allowed to criticise other cultures or religions for fear of offending them."

"Yeah it's a bit of a worry" Graham agreed. "And some of those religions and cultures have seriously flawed and even dangerous ideologies. Most religions claim to be the exclusive holders of the Truth, yet few of them are open to having their ideologies subjected to rational debate."

"Some will even try to kill you if you criticise them" Bill noted.

"Yeah, at least the philosophy department doesn't go quite that far" Graham grinned. "But many philosophers are also blinkered by their own atheist religion and don't welcome honest debate."

"Why do you reckon that is Graham? Are philosophy and religion essentially the same?"

"Well I guess they both have Truth as their ideal. Philosophy professes to use reason to derive the Truth, whereas religion claims it through revelation. In reality though, philosophers are also subject to prejudices, similar to those of religious folks. The main source of prejudice comes from their peer group. They all cling together and few are willing to speak outside the group think."

Bill nodded "I've come across that phenomenon in scientific fields too. Even if I produce irrefutable evidence contradicting a prevailing scientific theory, if I'm an outsider, those in authority in the field will not even consider the evidence. Instead they try to ridicule and discredit me."

"It's a human failing that even Socrates was conscious of Bill. He pointed out that we're influenced mostly by our own peer group. People will accept complete nonsense if it comes from one of their own whereas they're likely to reject an obvious truth if it's being delivered by an outsider. Truth is usually secondary to the will of the group."

"Why do you reckon that is?" Bill asked.

"I guess it's mainly the fear of being thrown out of the group."

"Yeah, I think you're right" Bill agreed. "So if most modern philosophers are atheists because of this group think phenomenon, where did the atheist thinking come from in the first place? I mean there must have been some individuals who started it."

"Sure, it's an interesting question. Of course there have been a number of influential atheists like Friedrich Nietzsche and Bertrand Russell. They were put off religion by the dogmas of their upbringing. They found it easy to deconstruct these dogmas and from there concluded that the whole idea of God is also false. But that was a huge leap of faith on their part."

"Or a huge leap of unfaith" Bill quipped.

"Yeah" Graham chuckled. "And once they've convinced themselves they become very passionate in their non-beliefs and want to convert others to their way of thinking. Because they're so convinced they're right they feel they can justify intellectual dishonesty. For example they tell us about wars that have been fought over religion and atrocities carried out by oppressive religious regimes yet they ignore the horrors of atheist regimes such as the French reign of terror and Stalinist Russia. People who are utterly convinced of their own self-righteousness can be very convincing you know Bill. Charismatic types can sway others purely through their own self-assured arrogance."

"Cult leaders" Bill nodded "in this case the cult of atheism. What would Plato have made of it do you think?"

"Well of course Plato fully believed in a Creator God. He perceived the order in the universe, the laws of nature and so on and reasoned that this order could not have come from random chance."

"So would Plato have thought that modern atheists are irrational?"

"Yes and I think so too" Graham replied. "To observe the perfect natural order of the universe and to believe that it could come from chaos by chance is absurd."

"Did Plato encounter atheists in his day?" Bill asked.

"Yes of course, atheism has always been around. He noted that young men in particular are inclined towards atheism. He observed their tendency to want to argue and debate everything, likening them to puppy dogs that love to pull everything apart for amusement. That kind of immature cantankerousness can lead to silly views that question our very senses, suggesting for example that you can never know anything is true or that we can't even prove that we exist."

"That sounds like nihilism" Bill remarked.

"Oh yes, it comes under all sorts of guises: nihilism, existentialism, logical positivism, postmodernism and philosophical scepticism. All these nonsensical doctrines try to undermine our ability to determine real Truth and to think rationally. They amount to philosophical bankruptcy."

"I guess it's the sort of thinking that's led to the so-called postmodern idea of relativism, that there is no right or wrong and that one culture or religion is equal to another" Bill suggested.

"Yes indeed, and it defies common sense and logic. Plato would have detested that sort of thinking. He fully trusted in our ability to reason and to figure out the truth for ourselves. He would admit that we can't be absolutely sure on some things, but by using our observations and powers of reason we can determine the most probable explanations. Once we have a reasonable view about the nature of existence he thought we ought to hang onto it, but not too passionately and be willing to let our convictions go if they're shown to be wrong."

Bill nodded "So what was Plato's view about the nature of our existence?"

"Well, having deduced that there is indeed a Creator, he then reasoned the Creator would have to be good and would desire everything He created also to be good as far as possible. He argued that God gave us intelligence and reason so we could figure out how to become good like Him and the free will to decide to be good or not. Our intelligence and free will are incorporated into our souls, which exist in a spirit world separate from the physical world and that live on after we die."

"That sounds like faith" Bill interrupted. "I mean we can't know for sure that there's a life for us after death."

"Of course, but it is faith based on reason. When Socrates was sentenced to death he wasn't afraid. He was fairly certain he was going somewhere good because he knew he had not done wrong. On the other hand he feared for the fate of his oppressors who obviously had done wrong in taking his life.

Socrates reasoned that because God is perfect and therefore just and that He gave us free will to choose right or wrong, there must be a system to reward our good behaviour and to punish the bad. If we didn't have to face the consequences of our actions we would never learn how to perfect our souls."

"So, according to Plato, is our objective to perfect our souls?" Bill asked.

"Yes absolutely" Graham replied.

"Did he think this was possible in one lifetime?"

"No he subscribed to the concept of reincarnation after the ideas of Orpheus."

"That's interesting" Bill nodded "How did he think we ought to perfect our souls?"

"Plato thought that God puts us in circumstances that enable us to learn the lessons we need to learn. For example Socrates thanked God for the gift of a shrewish wife because it enabled him to better cultivate the virtue of patience. He thought we should seek wisdom, in other words to figure out what's the right course of action and then to take that right course. He said that if we think hard and honestly, always seeking the Truth, through constant reflection and self-examination we will come to know what's right and that once we know what's right we will do it."

"That's a big call, that if we know what's right we will do it" Bill interjected.

"I guess Plato had an optimistic view of human nature" Graham nodded.

"Did that carry through into his politics too do you think?" Bill asked. "I mean I've heard that his views have inspired fascism and dictatorships because he didn't believe in democracy."

"Yes his authoritarian politics are often used to discredit him. His observations of the fledgling Athenian democracy led him to believe that a democratic society would be based purely on pleasure seeking, self-indulgence and individual greed and would lead to decadence and a loss of values."

"There might be some truth in that" Bill remarked. "When you look at our modern consumer society, we do seem to have lost some of our values that were originally based on Christian principles."

Graham nodded "Plato envisaged a society ruled by an elite class of specially educated and devoted "philosophers" that would uphold and live by noble moral standards and values. His idea of a philosopher though was more like what we would call a saint, someone who was totally devoted to the highest of principles and was completely unselfish."

"And that kind of person is hard to find" Bill quipped, "especially among the ruling classes."

"That's right. By definition, saintly people don't generally want to rule over others. Even the few that start out with noble intentions in time become corrupted by power and greed, particularly if they know they can't be voted out. We've seen it time and time again throughout history."

"It's great having the benefit of hindsight" Bill agreed. "Democracy might not be perfect but it seems to work the best. Plato's autocracy might work in theory, but in practice it leads to totalitarian regimes run by despotic tyrants."

Graham nodded "I guess Plato was an idealist. We can be taught to do what's right through education and by the example of great teachers like Socrates but in reality many of us will choose wrong even if we know what's right."

"Apart from figuring out what's right for ourselves" Bill continued, "Did Plato give any guidelines for what he thought was right?"

"Plato envisaged a system of perfect ideas or "Forms" in which goodness, justice and truth existed and that we should continually strive to know and then to practice. To him it was a mixture of seeking wisdom and practicing virtue. Virtues such as temperance, courage and justice are part of these perfect Forms.

"What did he mean by truth?" Bill asked.

"Plato differentiated between small truth and great Truth. We could distinguish the two by saying truth with a small "t" and Truth with a capital "T." Capital "T" Truth relates to the highest matters concerning the soul and is always vital whereas small "t" truth is relatively unimportant. For example he used myths in which the details could be untrue but they illustrate great Truths. Also he argued that it might be acceptable to tell lies in such cases as dealing with enemies or when a friend is about to do something harmful in a fit of madness."

"So lying might even be an act of love sometimes" Bill remarked. "I like that idea."

"Yes, and I guess you could simplify much of Plato's thinking down to that one word: Love."

Bill nodded "That seems to be the main message I'm getting from the main religions as well. Thank you for your help on this Graham, you've given me a lot to think about."

"Glad to help" Graham replied. "Perhaps you could send me a copy of your book when you've finished it."

"Absolutely."

Chapter 7—False Prophets

"Human beings are perhaps never more frightening than when they are convinced beyond doubt that they are right." Laurens van der Post

When Bill returned home from the University there was a message on his phone from a lady in New Zealand saying that his mother was very ill and would he please call her back. His mother was now quite elderly and had been ill from time to time so this was no great surprise. After phoning the lady, who turned out to be one of his mother's friends, he decided to book a flight to New Zealand as soon as possible. His mother hadn't said anything to him herself but she was a very proud and fiercely independent woman who would be unlikely to tell him, even if there was something was seriously wrong.

Within a few days he arrived in New Zealand, his country of birth. It turned out that Bill's mother had indeed been very ill but was now on the mend. After seeing that she was okay and making sure she had access to appropriate health services, Bill had a few days to spare before his booked flight home. He decided to get in touch with an old hunting and fishing buddy who suggested they could go into the bush for a couple of days.

Don was a mad keen deer hunter and spent most of his spare time in the bush. He said that he had a few things to tidy up at work and suggested Bill go around to his place to wait. He would ask his de-facto partner Akram to take a couple of pheasants out of the freezer for dinner that evening and they would set off the next day.

Bill had met Akram only once before, many years earlier. He didn't know much about her except that she was originally from Iran and had come to New Zealand following the Islamic revolution with her Iranian husband. They had a son together but were subsequently divorced. Her ex-husband had moved to Australia and she had stayed on in New Zealand to bring up her son. Don and Akram had now lived together for about ten years.

Akram greeted Bill warmly at the door and asked him to make himself at home. Don's house was much more homely than the rough bachelor pad that Bill remembered. "You've done the place up nicely" Bill complemented. "It needed a woman's touch."

"Thank you, would you like something to drink."

"I'd love a cup of tea" Bill replied.

"Oh that's marvellous" Akram replied warmly "I hardly ever have anyone to drink tea with, Don doesn't drink it."

"Yep that sounds like Don alright its either beer or coffee for him."

"You obviously know him well."

Bill laughed "Yeah we go back a long way."

As Bill sat down in the lounge he noticed an English translation of the Quran sitting prominently on the table.

"Are you still a practicing Muslim Akram?" he asked as she brought in a traditional Iranian tea set.

"Oh you know, not a very good one I'm afraid. But I have been reading the Quran lately."

"Islam is pretty unkind to women isn't it?" Bill asked bluntly. "I mean no offence but, as a woman, how do you feel about that side of it."

"I think it's a bit overblown" she replied. "There's a lot of stuff that goes on against women that isn't even in the Quran."

"But doesn't it say in the Quran that a man is allowed to beat his wife if she's disobedient?"

"Yes that's true" Akram conceded "and that's exactly what my ex-husband used to do to me. I'm not saying it's perfect but there are problems with other religions too, even in Christianity women are treated below men."

Bill nodded "That may be so, but it's a question of degree. In Islam a woman's testimony is worth only half that of a man's, which makes rape almost impossible to prosecute."

"I know what you mean" Akram agreed. "A woman can even incriminate herself by reporting a rape."

"And what about the polygamy that Islam allows, would you like it if Don had other wives?"

"We're not actually married but I'm sure *he* would like it" Akram grinned.

"But what if it was the other way around, that you had two husbands? I bet he wouldn't like that" Bill argued.

"I can't even cope with one" she laughed. Just then a car pulled up outside. "Oh that will be my son Alan home from university." The door opened and a young man of about twenty entered.

"Alan this is Bill an old friend of Don's."

"Gidday Bill" Alan nodded as he sat down next to his mother who poured him some tea. "What were you talking about?" he asked. "It sounded interesting."

"We were talking about sharia law" Akram responded.

"Oh I see" Alan said quizzically.

"Do you know much about it?" Bill asked.

"Only what I've heard from some of my Iraqi friends at University. It's the Islamic Law. Some of it seems okay like the fact that drinking and gambling are forbidden. That has to be a good thing when you look at all the trouble they cause in this country."

"In Australia too" Bill acknowledged. "But what about some of the barbaric penalties under sharia law like amputation of limbs for theft and death by stoning for adultery?"

"I guess if people don't steal or commit adultery it's not a problem" Alan replied. "I know some people who are Christian and they have some pretty weird ideas too. Who can say which religion is the right one?"

"I agree" Bill responded. "We can't say which religion is right but some might be more right than others don't you think?"

"Isn't that a bit racist?" Alan asked indignantly.

"I don't think it's racist" Bill responded. "I have no problem with the colour of anyone's skin. That's a genetic attribute. Races are equal, but religions and cultures aren't equal. Our race is something we're born into and we have no control over it, but our religion is our choice."

"Actually we don't have any choice about our religion in my home country" Akram interrupted. "We're born into our Muslim religion and basically we are forbidden to leave it or convert to another religion. It can even be punishable by death."

"But you're not in that country now" Bill replied. "You're in New Zealand and you can choose any religion you like."

"Are you trying to convert us to Christianity?" Akram asked teasingly.

"No because I know the penalty for that is death too" Bill laughed. "But seriously is a religion that preaches hate, violence and intolerance equal to one that preaches love, peace and forgiveness? I'm not saying Christianity has all the answers either, and I'm not a Christian myself in the conventional sense. But when we look at a religion I think we need to look first of all at the *example* of the founder. What sort of person were they and how did they behave towards their fellow man?"

"Know them by their fruits?" Akram suggested.

"Exactly" Bill continued "and when I compare what we know about the life of Christ or Buddha, for example, with what we know about the life of Muhammad, there's a big difference. In the case of Christ and Buddha, they lived humble and self-sacrificing lives devoted to love, peace and the welfare of others. Muhammad, on the other hand, was by all accounts a rather selfish warlord who spread his own religion by violent military conquest."

Alan's expression seemed to harden and there was an awkward silence.

Finally Akram broke the silence "Actually I think that's how Islam came into our country too. The invading Arabs brought it in and Islam took over from the national religion of Persia that was Zoroastrianism."

"Yes and I believe Zoroastrianism was also founded by a man devoted to peace, moral excellence and ethical behaviour" Bill added.

"Zarathustra" Akram nodded "He taught us the motto: good thoughts, good words and good deeds and he preached the golden rule: not to do to others anything that doesn't seem good to oneself."

"But Islam has the golden rule too doesn't it Mum?" Alan interrupted.

"I'm not sure, I think so" Akram replied hesitantly.

"I'd be grateful if you could look that up for me" Bill said. "I'm doing some research on religions for a book I'm writing and I'd like to know what the moral teachings of Muhammad actually are."

"Perhaps you could do that for Bill" Akram suggested. "You have your books and the internet."

"OK I can do that" Alan agreed and went to his room.

Shortly later Don got home from work and greeted Bill amiably. "Let's go up to the RSA" he said "while we're waiting for dinner."

At the Returned Servicemen's Association club they enjoyed a game of snooker and a beer while catching up on each other's news. Don boasted the results of his latest hunting trip as he was inclined to do. "We're all set to go tomorrow" he added. "It's still the roar so we might find a stag if we're lucky. I hope you don't mind but I've asked young Alan to come along with us."

"Not at all, he seems like a nice young fella and very intelligent too."

"Yeah he is that alright. To tell you the truth I wouldn't mind if you had a chat to him about his religion, because I know it's a speciality of yours. He seems to be hanging around more and more with some young Muslim lads that I don't like the look of. I mean I'm sure they're fine but you read about young Muslim blokes that get influenced by some crazy ideas and the next thing you know they're strapping on a suicide bomb or something."

Bill nodded "Sure I can do that if the opportunity arises. He's certainly at that vulnerable age where peer pressure can be extreme. Young men can do some pretty silly things just to impress their friends."

"Like we did" Don remarked as he sank the black.

"Yeah" Bill laughed. "But what you really need to watch out for is if he's being exposed to extremist ideology. Young people who've become a bit alienated from mainstream society are an easy target for extremist religious leaders. They offer young people a sense of purpose and "belonging" that many people crave. Religious leaders also have authority and power in their local community and so can be very influential to gullible young people."

On returning to Don's house they enjoyed a delicious dinner that Akram had cooked while Don gave a blow by blow account of the hunt that resulted in the shooting of these magnificent birds. The next morning they set off very early in Don's ute on the four hour drive to a national park near Taupo. On arrival they offloaded Don's quad bike from the ute. "Jump on" Don said to Bill when they had loaded on their gear.

"What about Alan?" Bill asked. The four wheel motorbike was fully loaded and it was obvious there was no room for a third person.

"He can run" Don chuckled. "He's young, besides he needs the exercise."

Alan grinned back "Don't worry I'm used to it" he said meekly and waved as they raced off.

There was a sign at the start of the track that said "Walking track only, No motorbikes, No dogs." When Bill pointed to the sign Don just laughed and whistled to his dog. "He hasn't changed" Bill chortled to himself under his breath. Signs like this were a minor irrelevant detail to Don who had frequented this bush since he was a youth.

Bill clung on for dear life as Don sped along the track through the bush that was in places overgrown and full of deep ruts. They were constantly being slapped by branches and at one point Don lost control of the vehicle and they both ended up on the ground with the bike on top of them. Amazingly they were uninjured and Don leapt back on the bike as if nothing had happened.

After about half an hour they reached the end of the track that could be negotiated by the bike. "Right we'll have a coffee while we're waiting" Don said. "Give me a hand to hide the bike in the bush."

They boiled the billy and waited for Alan. "Don't worry, we've only got a couple of hours walk from here" Don teased as Alan finally jogged towards them puffing and gasping.

The hike to the place where they were to camp the night was quite steep and exhausting but very enjoyable for Bill. It brought back old memories and he realised there were things about his old country that he missed. Their destination turned out to be a campsite consisting of a large hollow log that had a piece of plastic draped over it weighted down by dirt and rocks. "Is that where we're sleeping?" Bill asked apprehensively.

Don laughed "Sure is."

Bill shuddered as he looked into the deep recesses of the dank rotting log that was so big that several people could indeed sleep inside rather snuggly. My God he thought, if this was Australia you'd never risk even going into a dark hollow log like this let alone sleep in it. It would probably be infested by poisonous spiders and centipedes at least and at worst poisonous snakes. But this was New Zealand and there were of course no such nasty creatures, he rationalised.

After cooking and enjoying a hearty feast and being entertained by Don's stories of other hunting adventures, it was getting dark and they decided to retire as the plan was to be hunting at dawn the next morning.

"I'll sleep right in there at the top end" Don announced. "There are cave wetas close to your face up there but the odd bite won't worry me."

Bill and Alan readily nodded their agreement as they laid their sleeping bags out in the roomier open end of the log. The weta was the one insect that could inspire fear in the heart of the average squeamish New Zealander. They were quite large and ugly creatures and were reputed to bite but Bill had never heard of anyone who had actually been bitten.

When they lay down Bill looked up to see that the so-called cave wetas were in fact harmless looking grasshoppers and he drifted off to sleep.

He woke up to the sound of Alan's voice complaining about having a wet sleeping bag. It was pouring with rain. Bill rolled over "Oh hell my bag is wet too" he said as he felt the water pooling around his legs.

Don was still snoring peacefully. "Now I know why he wanted that end of the log" Bill remarked. "It's as dry as toast up there."

"Yeah" Alan laughed "He knows how to look after himself."

"How about I light the gas cooker and make us a cup of tea" Bill suggested. "That'll warm us up."

"Sounds good" Alan agreed "I'll see if I can find a dry towel."

"Did you have a chance to look up that stuff about morality in Islam?" Bill asked as they waited for the billy to boil.

"Yeah I did a bit."

"And what did you find?"

"Well I didn't find the golden rule specifically but I found some stuff I thought was like it, such as that we should do what's right and avoid what's evil."

"But how do you tell what is right and what's evil?" Bill asked. "Does it say in the Quran?"

"Well there are some principles like charity to the poor and being fair and honest in your dealings with others."

"I wonder though, does that apply to your dealings with everyone or just towards other Muslim believers?" Bill enquired.

"I'm not sure" Alan responded "I hadn't really thought about it."

"The reason I ask is that I know there are Islamic teachings about fighting and killing nonbelievers."

"Could be" Alan nodded. The billy had boiled and Bill poured the tea.

They drank in silence for a while before Bill continued his questions "So what does it take to be a Muslim?"

"You have to confess there is no God but God and that Muhammad is the true and final messenger of God."

"Is that it?"

"Pretty much yes, Islam means submission and you must submit yourself to this belief and to the will of God."

"So if you have to submit to the will of God does that mean a Muslim has no free will?" Bill asked.

"I guess it does."

"But do you believe in some kind of judgement where you will go to heaven or hell?"

"Yes of course."

"So if you think everything is God's will then how can you have any influence on whether you go to heaven or hell?"

"It's a bit confusing" Alan responded.

"Confusing and inconsistent" Bill continued. "If you believe you can influence whether or not you will go to heaven or hell by choosing right or wrong, then you must believe in free will."

Alan became tense and said with annoyance "All I know is that Muhammad is the true and final Prophet of God."

"So does that mean you have to accept the Quran is the absolute and final last word of God, without question?" Bill asked.

"Yes absolutely and without question. There is no flexibility in the word of God."

"What makes you think it really is the word of God?"

"It just *is* the word of God revealed to Prophet Muhammad. That's what I believe."

"But how do you know for sure that Muhammad was God's true prophet. I mean there've been many others who've also claimed to have received the revealed truth of God through visions, dreams, or conversations with God. Even today there are people alive who claim to talk to God. Almost every religion has been started by someone claiming revelation from God. How do you know the revelations to Muhammad are right and all these other ones are wrong?"

"I . . . I don't know" Alan stammered. "It's our religion you're not allowed to mock it."

"I'm not mocking it, I'm just questioning it."

"Well that's not allowed either, you aren't allowed to question or criticise Islam."

Bill nodded "Do you think it's a good thing that no one is allowed to criticise your religion?"

"It's insulting to criticise it" Alan responded.

"But if you can't criticise it how can anything improve?"

Alan shook his head "You can't improve it if it's the word of God."

Bill scratched his chin thoughtfully before continuing "That used to be the prevailing attitude in Christianity too in the Middle Ages. In those days you could be tortured or even burned at the stake if you criticised the "official" Christianity. That situation suited those in power. By preventing any criticism the status quo is maintained and that ensures the authority of those already in control. In that case it was the Pope and his Bishops in partnership with the aristocratic kings. I think you also have religious leaders now with high status who benefit from the status quo."

"We Shi'ites have the Imams and the Sunnis have their Muftis" Alan agreed.

Bill continued "When you have a belief system that says everything that's in this book is the absolute Truth you have a problem. Religious leaders can point to this paragraph or that sentence and use it to further their own agendas. In the Christian world nothing really improved until the freethinking of the enlightenment and the struggle that ended in the separation of Church and State, so that reason could finally prevail over religious authority. Christianity still has its fundamentalist leaders but they no longer have power over anyone except their own congregation because of the separation of religion from the State."

"Maybe Islam will have its own enlightenment" Alan said rubbing his eyes. The rain had finally stopped and they were both able to get back to sleep. It didn't seem long before Don's alarm went off and he was pushing past them to get out into the darkness. "I'll put the coffee on" he said.

Bill dragged himself up and shook the water out of his sleeping bag. "Did you get wet?" Don asked. "That's bad luck, I slept like a log."

Bill winked at Alan who grinned back. They soon cheered up as the grey of dawn arrived and it was time to start the hunt. There were two rifles and the arrangement was that Bill and Alan would take turns with the second rifle.

They walked for about an hour through the bush without any fresh sign of deer until suddenly things changed. There was fresh deer scat on the ground, very fresh. Don put his finger to his lips and whispered for Bill and Alan to go one way around the ridge in front of them and he would go around the other.

It was Bill's turn with the rifle and just after they parted ways he caught sight of a red brown shape ahead through the trees. He put his hand up motioning for Alan to stay put behind him while he moved around a group of trees to get a better view. Sure enough, looking from the improved angle, Bill could clearly see a stag, as well as several other deer that were slightly obscured about eighty meters away grazing in a clearing.

Bill raised the rifle slowly and deliberately, taking aim at the head of the stag that he could now see clearly through the telescopic sight. He was just about to squeeze the trigger when there was a loud shout. Don was yelling at his dog. The deer were gone in a flash. As Bill lowered the rifle a brief moment of annoyance was quickly replaced by an unexpected feeling of relief. Perhaps the killer instinct from his youth had faded. He smiled knowing the stag would live to graze another day, or at least until Don saw it.

He turned back towards Alan who had remained motionless and silent. "Anything?" he asked quietly.

"No nothing" Bill smiled. "I thought I saw something through the trees but it turned out to be nothing after all. It must be your turn with the rifle."

They hunted the rest of the day without success until nearly dusk and they were again close to camp. "You guys go and get the fire going" Don said. "I just want to have a quick look in this valley and I'll see you back at the camp."

It was almost dark as Bill and Alan arrived back at the hollow log and just as they were lighting the fire they heard a shot. About fifteen minutes later Don turned up grinning from ear to ear. "Well come and help me with the bloody thing!" he said gruffly.

With the help of torches and the now useful dog they managed to relocate the deer that Don had dragged to the track. They lugged the carcass of the large red hind back to camp.

The second night in the hollow log turned out to be much more comfortable than the first. Exhausted, they all slept soundly. In the morning after taking some photos of Don with his deer and rifle it came time to head home. "Aren't you going to butcher that thing before we go?" Bill asked.

"Nah I reckon we'll have a go at taking it out whole" Don said. "I reckon we could string it on a pole and we could carry it between two of us."

"Have you done that before?"

"Well no but I've seen it done in the movies" Don replied. He cut a stout pole and they strung the animal's feet front and back to the pole. Don hoisted one end of the pole over his shoulder and Bill took the rear. At first it seemed to work quite well but when they got to the first downslope they struck a problem. The carcass took on a side to side swinging momentum that soon became so uncontrollable that it rendered them both in a heap at the bottom of the slippery slope in a tangle of limbs and dead deer.

Alan, who was watching from behind, was in fits of laughter. After the initial shock both Bill and Don soon realised the comedy of their situation and joined in the mirth. From then on they took it more steadily and eventually arrived back at the main track where the bike was hidden. This time Don somehow managed to stack the bike so that all three of them along with the deer and all their gear fitted on.

The ride back was even more hair-raising than the ride out because of the additional load. Just before they reached the road where the ute was parked Don screeched the bike to a halt. In front of them, where previously there had been a perfectly good track, there was now a large deep moat, completely impassable. There was no way around it and the water was very deep.

"The bastards!" Don yelled. "They must have seen our tracks." He explained that the Department of Conservation had obviously been in with an excavator to deliberately stop quad bikes from getting through and specifically to stop this one from getting home.

It turned out however that Don was well prepared for such an eventuality, which apparently had happened to him before. Using a chainsaw that was hidden in his ute, within an hour they had built a passable bridge and were able, with the help of a winch, to get the bike up the sheer sides of the cliff carved by the excavator.

Finally, they re-loaded their gear onto the ute and set off. Just up the road they passed a large Department of Conservation excavator that was being loaded onto a truck. They lowered their heads as they raced past it.

Chapter 8—Return to Egypt

"The Truth is a pure heart and a blameless life, and not a set of dogmas and opinions" James Allen

On Bill's return from New Zealand there was a promotional email from his travel agent in his inbox. Ordinarily he would immediately delete such items but there was something about this one that caught his attention. It was an advertisement for discount airfares to the Middle East. He had never been to the Holy Land and he thought this would be a great opportunity to visit the birth place of the Abrahamic religions and would also enable him to return to Egypt, where he had unfinished business.

Sarah had always wanted to visit the Holy sites of Christianity and readily agreed when Bill suggested they make the trip. They rescheduled some other plans and within a few weeks they were on their way.

Bill was apprehensive about travelling in Egypt as the country was still in political turmoil following the uprising that had led to the ousting of the long-term dictator Mubarak. The country was now operating under a fledgling democracy that was dominated by Islamic parties. It had been the second country to succumb to the so-called "Arab spring" that had seen both Tunisia and Libya oust their dictator regimes lured by the promise of democratic rule.

Bill had arranged for them to visit the Giza Plateau on their first day, with Angela who was now working for a travel company in Cairo. When he had mentioned this to Sarah she had smiled and said that would be nice but Bill could sense some tension in her voice. He had thought hard about whether it was a good idea to contact Angela, but in the end he rationalised that she was his friend and after all, her knowledge of Egypt would be a great asset to them. He was apprehensive as they waited in their hotel lobby for her to arrive. He hardly recognised her when she finally entered the lobby wearing dark glasses and a hijab style headscarf that made her look like an Egyptian. It's so lovely to see you both" she said as she hugged them both warmly in turn, giving Bill a deliberate kiss on the cheek."

"You look the part" Bill said as he stood back to admire her.

"Oh yes, I've learned its best to look like a local around here" she smiled. "Our car is waiting. Are you ready to go?"

Angela had arranged for a vehicle from her company with a driver to take them to the Giza Plateau. She ushered them into the back seat and then took the front next to the Egyptian driver with whom she spoke in Arabic."

"Wow that's impressive" Bill remarked. "You speak Arabic now?"

"Oh thanks, just enough to get by" she replied modestly.

"What does your job here entail?" Sarah enquired.

"Our company specialises in new age groups. For example I take groups to the Great Pyramid to meditate. We also conduct discussion groups and seminars covering alternative theories about ancient Egypt, the pyramids and so on."

"You mean theories about ancient civilisations and that kind of thing?" Bill asked.

"Sure, amongst others."

"That sounds interesting and would suit you pretty well I think" Bill added, "But I'm surprised the Egyptian authorities let you get away with it. Aren't they pretty sensitive about that kind of thing?"

Angela nodded "The authorities don't like us but they tolerate us because we bring them heaps of money. We keep a low profile and the meditation is all very discrete."

"So there wouldn't be any chanting with the meditation" Bill chirped cheekily.

"No chanting at all" Angela laughed.

It was only a short drive to the Giza plateau and they were soon disembarking onto what was now quite familiar territory to Bill. However, this second visit was no less awe-inspiring than the first. He marvelled at the sight of the Great Pyramid and its lesser partners towering skyward from the desert sands. "Imagine how magnificent it all must have looked in its heyday" Bill remarked "when the pyramids still had their polished encasing."

Angela took them on a tour around the plateau, talking almost non-stop. She often had to snap sternly in Arabic to deter the endless number of opportunists who aggressively offered camel rides and souvenirs. It struck Bill that there were very few tourists compared to his previous visit and when he commented on this Angela explained that the tourism industry had taken a severe hit since the so-called revolution.

Finally they approached the entrance to the Great Pyramid. "In theory they won't let me go in with you because I'm a tour guide, but sometimes I can slip past them" Angela said quietly as she removed her headscarf, shook her hair loose and changed her glasses. "Hold my hand as if we're together" she whispered to Bill. He felt the soft skin of her hand as she squeezed his fingers enticingly. He looked awkwardly towards Sarah but she appeared to take no notice as she stepped in front of them. Bill passed their tickets to the guards and they walked through the entrance without incident.

As they climbed up the steep ascending passage Bill began to expound his theory about the purpose of the Great Pyramid to Angela. Sarah had heard it all before but still listened intently. "The Subterranean Chamber is rough and unfinished looking" he explained "which led Egyptologists to believe that it had originally been planned as the Pharaoh's tomb but was abandoned for a preferred option higher in the pyramid. The funny thing is that the ceiling is smooth and finished. So my theory is that this represents man in his raw state, when he has first begun on the path to enlightenment. The way up from the Subterranean Chamber is an incredibly steep and difficult so-called workers shaft that represents the hard and disciplined road man must travel towards the attainment of wisdom and virtue.

The second level or so-called Queen's Chamber is completely finished except the floor is rough. This represents the man that is well on the road to enlightenment, but the rough floor indicates that he is not quite complete. Then finally the march upward through the glorious grand gallery to the perfect so-called King's Chamber represents the final and highest level of attainment where man has perfected his soul."

"So do you think rituals took place here?" Angela asked as they finally entered the wondrous King's Chamber.

"Yes I think so" Bill replied. "In fact I think ceremonies would have taken place in all three chambers, but a ceremony here would have been a rare event. This inner sanctum I believe was reserved for very special occasions."

They stood in silent wonder, picturing the scene of a solemn ceremony taking place thousands of years ago in this very room. The only feature was the so-called sarcophagus standing at the far end of the room.

"How do you think the sarcophagus was used in the ceremony?" Angela asked.

"I can only speculate" Bill responded. "I've heard one interesting theory that the granite coffer was used to house the Ark of the Covenant."

"I've heard that theory too" Angela nodded, "but I thought the Ark of the Covenant was built by Moses to house the sacred tablets of the Ten Commandments, and of course, Moses didn't come along until more than a thousand years later."

"Yes" Bill replied "but this theory holds that the Ark of the Covenant contained sacred relics from an ancient civilisation. The story goes that this Pyramid was built by members of a secret religion surviving from that civilisation. The religion continued right up until the time of Moses when he took the remaining people of the religion along with the Ark from Egypt to Jerusalem."

"Was it the ancient civilisation of Atlantis?" Angela asked excitedly.

"That's what the story says" Bill nodded. Just then a large tour group entered the chamber and they decided it was time to leave.

That evening Angela joined them both for dinner at the rooftop restaurant of their five-star hotel, which overlooked the pyramids. There were so few people staying in the hotel that they were the only ones at the restaurant.

"It's not like it used to be" Angela remarked. "Look out on that street" she pointed to the noisy throng of activity outside the high impenetrable walls of the hotel that resembled the walls of a prison.

"Notice, not a single woman without a hijab, men mostly wearing robes, not a tourist in site. You just wouldn't go out there now as a tourist."

"Yes that's amazing" Bill agreed. "When I was last here there were tourists everywhere out on that very street."

"The change has been dramatic" Angela nodded "and I don't see it changing back any time soon with the Islamists in power."

Angela talked about her life in Cairo which seemed to be rather lonely. The conversation turned to her love life which she said was non-existent. "I never thought I would want to have children" she said "but now I'm not so sure. I've heard of this biological clock thing. I never believed it but now I'm over forty I have this real yearning you know. But the men I meet all seem to be divorced and most have already had their children and don't want to start again."

When Sarah went to the bathroom Angela and Bill stared into each other's eyes. She looked like she was about to say something but Bill was first to speak. "Angela you're so lovely. I know you'll find someone and if you're meant to have children you will." Angela's eye's moistened as she broke her gaze. When Sarah returned she looked at them quizzically but said nothing.

When the time came to say goodbye, Angela manoeuvred Bill aside, hugged him firmly, kissing him briefly but tantalisingly on the lips.

Back in their hotel room Sarah said "I guess at times like this you wish you were a Muslim."

"What do you mean?" Bill stammered.

"Well they're allowed more than one wife aren't they?" Sarah retorted teasingly.

"Oh yeah they have that pretty well sorted don't they" Bill chuckled, "but I don't think you'd like that."

"There would be bloodshed, I assure you" Sarah asserted.

"Just as well I'm not a Muslim then" Bill grinned.

They had arranged on the following day to visit the Cairo Museum as well as the ancient Christian sector know as Coptic Cairo. The shuttle bus from the hotel dropped them outside the

Museum where they met their guide, a pleasant young man who introduced himself as Bishoy. He was amazingly knowledgeable and had them enthralled as he took them through the various displays of artefacts and statues. The spectacular array of immaculately preserved objects found in Tutankhamen's tomb provided a rare glimpse into the ancient world.

But it was the section devoted to the reign of Tutankhamen's father Akhenaton, the mysterious heretic Pharaoh that was of much greater interest to Bill. Bishoy showed little interest in this section and Bill was pleased when he suggested they could spend some time looking around the museum on their own and he would meet them outside in an hour.

Bill found the layout of the museum to be quite confusing. "No wonder they need guides" he muttered as he tried to get his bearings. He suddenly noticed that Sarah was no longer with him. He called her name, and looked around apprehensively. There were no guides around or even English-speaking people. The recent violent anti-American demonstrations outside the museum had discouraged tourists.

Then, to his relief he finally heard her call out "Bill come and look at this."

He followed the sound of her voice and found her next to a large granite slab covered in hieroglyphs. "The caption says this is the Israel Stele" Sarah said.

"Wow, how did you find this?" Bill exclaimed excitedly. "It's just tucked away here with all this other junk; I would never have found it."

"Just lucky I guess" Sarah smiled, "what does it mean though."

"It's highly significant" Bill replied. "The last two lines apparently refer to the Pharaoh Merneptah's victory against several groups in Canaan including Israel. This is the first mention of the name Israel in the archaeological record. So what that means is that the exodus had to be before 1208 BC, which is when this was written."

"So when was the exodus then?" Sarah asked.

"Well there's still a lot of debate about that" Bill replied "but most believe that it had to be after the start of the reign of Ramses

II who ruled from 1279 to 1213 BC. That's because there is a city of Raamses named in the Bible (Exodus 1.11), which is believed to be named after Ramses II."

"So the exodus had to be between 1279 and 1208 BC" Sarah commented.

"Yes I think so" Bill nodded.

"So how does that fit in with Egyptian history then?" Sarah continued. "Was there any mention of the exodus of the Israelites by the Egyptians and how does it fit in with that stuff about Akhenaton you've talked about?"

Sarah had often heard Bill talk about Akhenaton and his possible connection with Moses, but she had always been confused about dates and events before. Now, in the context of the history that was before her eyes, it had much more meaning and she now needed explanations that made sense.

"Come with me" Bill grinned taking Sarah by the hand and leading her to the section devoted to the reign of Akhenaton, that Bishoy had earlier glossed over.

"He was a bizarre looking character" Sarah commented pointing to the large statue depicting Akhenaton with a strange narrow face and wide feminine hips.

"I don't think he really looked like that" Bill laughed. "I think those weird depictions have some symbolic meaning, but when you look at these smaller statues of him they depict quite an ordinary looking person."

"Yes" Sarah responded "so what's your theory about the connection between Akhenaton and Moses?"

"Well for a start they're linked by their approximate dates in time and they're both credited with being the first monotheists."

"But weren't their religions quite different?" Sarah interrupted. "I thought Bishoy said that Akhenaton worshipped the Sun God."

"Yes but he didn't worship the sun itself, but rather an all-powerful invisible Creator God whose power was manifested in the sun. When you look at the fragments from what remains of Akhenaton's writings, his description of God bears a strong resemblance to the God of Moses. In fact there's such a strong similarity between Akhenaton's Hymn and the Aten and Psalm 104 that many people believe they were written by the same person."

"So what do you think was their relationship to each other?" Sarah asked.

"Well some people have suggested that Moses and Akhenaton were contemporaries or even that they are one and the same person. But I don't go along with that. If the dates we discussed before are correct, Moses came a hundred years or so after Akhenaton."

"Could those dates be wrong?" Sarah asked.

"Of course it's not possible to say for sure because the only account we have of Moses is the Biblical account and that doesn't have the name of an Egyptian Pharaoh that could match the timing with Egyptian history. In fact some people reject the very idea that Moses even existed because they say there is no story in Egyptian history that matches the Biblical account of an enslaved race of Israelites making an exodus from Egypt."

"But that doesn't mean it didn't happen" Sarah remarked. "History is always biased towards the people writing it. Historians are inclined to leave out stories that don't match their politics or beliefs or show themselves in a bad light."

"Absolutely" Bill agreed. "In fact it's a wonder we know anything at all about Akhenaton. The priesthood hated him for disbanding their lucrative religion and taking away their power. So much so that they tried to remove all trace of him from their history. But, in this case, I don't think the account of the enslavement and the exodus is actually missing from Egyptian history. It's right under our noses."

"Go on, I'm intrigued" Sarah said enthusiastically.

"Well there is a very well documented account in Egyptian history of a race of people that came to Egypt from the land of Canaan, which is basically the land of Israel and where the Biblical Joseph was from. This race of people came gradually to Egypt over a number of centuries. Many of them were skilled in mathematics, engineering and administration. They integrated so well into Egyptian society that they eventually became governors and even for a time Pharaohs. They were the 15th dynasty Pharaohs who ruled Egypt from 1620 to 1540 BC."

"The Hyksos!" Sarah exclaimed "The ones Bishoy said were the foreign rulers. You think the Israelites were the Hyksos?"

"Yes I think they are one and the same people."

"So why isn't that idea widely accepted?" Sarah asked.

"Well of course anyone coming from a Jewish or even Christian perspective is usually trying to prove Biblical "truths." So they tend to reject anything that doesn't correspond with an exact word for word Biblical account. But the Biblical account was recorded much later and is likely to contain factual errors due to the passage of time. It obviously contains a fair bit of mythical legend. Some of it is contradictory and even fanciful. Stories like Noah's flood, the parting of the Red Sea and so on, we need to take all that with a grain of salt. Then, on the other hand, we have the Egyptian account which is indeed historical, but of course the Egyptians were the eventual conquerors of the Hyksos and obviously wrote their bias into history."

"So you're saying that we can't rely one hundred per cent on either account."

"No, but the interesting thing is that the best known of all early Jewish historians Josephus actually did believe that the Hyksos were his ancestors. He thought that the exodus equated with the "expulsion" of the Hyksos by the Pharaoh Ahmose about 1560 BC. The problem with this idea though for more recent investigators is the timing. The date of the documented expulsion of the Hyksos rulers is several hundred years too early to be equated with the exodus.

But I think there's a simple explanation for this. Let's accept that the Hyksos leaders were defeated and either killed or expelled by Ahmose. But surely there were numerous Hyksos common people who remained. Isn't it likely that these people would have been enslaved, once their leaders had been ousted? I think the Hyksos people became enslaved at the beginning of the 18th Dynasty when their leaders were defeated by Ahmose. By the time of Akhenaton a couple of hundred years later they were the enslaved race mentioned in the Bible. This period of enslavement continued until the eventual exodus under Moses."

"So" Sarah said "are you suggesting that the Hyksos brought their monotheist religion with them and it was that religion that was adopted by Akhenaton and he wanted to make it the official religion."

"Yes."

"But how do you explain that there's no record of this?"

"There's no "official" record" Bill responded. "But, being a heretical religion that was a threat to the Egyptian Priesthood, it had to be kept secret. It operated underground. Like many religions through history that have continued esoterically, even today."

"And so after the Egyptian Priesthood got the better of Akhenaton the religion went back underground until the time of Moses?" Sarah asked.

"Yes I think so" Bill replied looking at his watch. "We don't have much time and there's one more thing I really want to see. Something that's much older."

They hurried back along the ground floor of the museum looking for old kingdom displays until finally Bill stopped in front of a small ivory statue in a glass case. "This is it!" he exclaimed excitedly. "This is the only known statue of Khufu the Pharaoh, who supposedly built the Great Pyramid."

"Such a tiny little statue" Sarah remarked studying the statue carefully "He doesn't look like the kind of guy who would build that gigantic monument for himself as a tomb does he?"

"No he doesn't" Bill agreed. "We'd better go."

After the museum they had lunch at a café, during which Sarah asked Bishoy how things were working out in Egypt under the new regime since the so-called revolution. Bishoy pretended not to hear but said quietly, almost in a whisper "later, we can't talk here."

As arranged, following lunch they went to Coptic Cairo. As soon as they had passed through the heavily guarded gates to the complex, Bishoy's attitude seemed to change completely. His voice became more confident and he appeared to relax. It became obvious that he was himself a Coptic Christian. Here, he was with his own people and was obviously well known. Everyone seemed to smile at him and greet him warmly. He took great pride in showing them the famous

Hanging Church and the Saints Sergius and Bacchus Church, where tradition has it that the Holy Family with the baby Jesus rested on their arrival in Egypt. He explained in great detail and with obvious pride the history of the Coptic Christian community in Egypt and their struggles against persecution and oppression through fifteen centuries following the Muslim invasion.

"Yes, Hillary Clinton was here" he said pointing to a photo on the wall of a souvenir shop picturing her alongside the owner of the establishment. "Now that she's the US Secretary of State I hope she remembers us. We might need help from the American people soon. You asked me about the revolution, well things are looking grim for us Copts. They burn our churches and when we protest . . ." Bishoy hesitated. "They slaughter us" he continued grimly, tears welling up in his eyes "Forgive me but my brother was killed recently during a protest."

"Sorry" Bill said sympathetically, "it must be a tough time for you. Is there any hope things might improve?"

"I'd love to think so but I doubt it very much. If anything it seems to be getting worse. My father is a doctor and he's just had his house burned down. Mubarak was a dictator but at least we had some protection under his regime. We're worried about the Muslim brotherhood that has taken over; I fear we'll be out of the frying pan and into the fire."

"Can there ever be a secular democracy in Egypt?" Bill asked.

Bishoy shook his head "It can only happen if there's a true separation of religion from State and I'm not sure if that's possible when Islamic parties dominate the Government. I'm not very encouraged when I look around at other Muslim countries that have regressed in recent times to fundamentalist Muslim rule. Look at Iran for example. Can true democracy ever happen in a country where reason is always trumped by religious dogma and when no one is allowed to criticise the dogma? You only need to look at what's happening in Libya and Tunisia. Libya has been liberated from a tyrant dictator but the first thing the new regime announces is that they're reintroducing sharia law and bringing back polygamy."

"For both men and women?" Sarah quipped.

"Of course" Bishoy laughed sarcastically. "In Tunisia too the Islamic parties dominate the new government. Heaven knows what will happen there. I fear their newfound freedom will be short-lived once the Islamic leaders begin to take control."

"What about Egypt though?" Bill asked "Can the Coptic Christians have any influence here?"

"What can we do? We're only ten per cent of the population" Bishoy replied. "I'm very worried about our future."

Bishoy escorted them back to their shuttle bus and wished them well for the remainder of their journey. The bus took them through some of the poorer parts of Cairo in which they were able to see the squalor in which most of the population lived. The filth in the streets was appalling. In one place they passed a dead horse that had simply been left to rot on the street by the canal. They saw huge queues for diesel fuel and an even longer one for cooking gas in which a violent street fight was being played out. Watching from the bus it seemed like a violent movie, but this was real.

Chapter 9—The Temple

"You seem to consider not whether a thing is or is not true, but who the speaker is and what country the tale comes from." Socrates

After a brief tour of Jordan, Bill and Sarah crossed the border into Israel and were transported by taxi to Tel Aviv. The first thing Bill noticed was how small the country was and how desolate, although to their credit, the Israelis had transformed much of the desert into good agricultural land with irrigation.

After a night in Tel Aviv they joined their tour. They had never been on a bus tour before, always preferring to travel independently under their own steam. However at this time, in this part of the world they were quite happy to be in a tour group. The bus headed south along the coast and turned inland near the border with the infamous Hamas controlled Palestinian state of Gaza. The Israeli guide announced that on a monthly (or sometimes weekly) basis, they would shoot rockets into the town of Ashkelon, through which they were now passing. "Don't worry though" he joked "I promised my wife I would get home safely, so you will be fine."

The tour bus was comfortable and well air conditioned, which was a welcome relief from the scorching desert sun. There was an air of excitement among the group of about a dozen people from various backgrounds, mainly Christians, who were here in the Holy Land on a once in a lifetime pilgrimage. In the seats across the aisle was another couple of about the same age as Bill and Sarah with whom they were soon chatting like old friends. Their names were Ben and Rachel. They were a Jewish couple from Belgium and they were doing this tour of Israel for the first time although Ben had spent some time working here on a kibbutz in his youth.

Bill thought it was a happy coincidence to be sitting next to some Jewish people, a religion he had not yet investigated, and he took the opportunity to steer the conversation to religion. It turned out that Ben was very knowledgeable about Judaism and enthusiastically answered Bill's questions. They became so engrossed in conversation that they decided to swap seats to more easily converse while the women were able to talk about other things.

"We're not devout religious folks" Ben explained "But as with most Israelis, our cultural heritage is important. Judaism is specific to the Jewish people and is more like an ethnic culture concerned with protecting the nation of Israel than it is a religion. Of course we have our fundamentalists too but they're a small minority. The association with the land of Israel is important to all of us though."

"Does that go back to the promise God supposedly made to Abraham?" Bill interrupted.

"Yes, I suppose so" Ben agreed. "Of course that promise has caused problems ever since and continues to do so, especially with the Muslim population."

Bill nodded "So what's the history of the relationship between Judaism and Islam?"

"There's a fierce rivalry that goes way back to the two sons of Abraham. We Jews believe our history and traditions came from Abraham's son Isaac and the Muslims believe theirs comes from his half-brother Ishmael, which is a little bit strange because Islam only developed fairly recently compared to Judaism. We believe we are the chosen people and so do they. It's a huge problem."

"But you do have the father Abraham in common" Bill interrupted.

"Yes we do, but the story of Abraham is not very helpful. I mean the idea that a loving God would test Abraham by asking him to kill his own son and then telling him to stop at the last minute; that's a pretty weird story."

"I guess that's where the idea of submission to the will of God comes from" Bill suggested.

Ben nodded "Unfortunately I think you're right. Our saving grace is that most of us don't take submission seriously anymore, unlike the Muslims. At the end of the day though, Judaism is the parent religion of all monotheism, both Christianity and Islam" Ben continued. "You could even consider them as schisms of the same religion."

"Like Mormonism is to Christianity" Bill suggested.

"Sure why not? Judaism has always had its schisms. Even in Christ's day there were the Pharisees, the Sadducees, the Essenes and so on. Jews have spread around the world and the range of beliefs today is quite diverse. The religion has been quite dynamic and flexible with the times."

"But surely Jews have some core beliefs in common."

"Well yes, we are all monotheists and of course we have the Ten Commandments. There are also a whole pile of other laws of behaviour too. A group of Rabbis came up with 613 commandments or rules for us to follow from the Torah."

"Wow; that sounds like a lot."

Ben grinned "Yeah I don't think many Jews these days would even know what they are, let alone follow them. Most of us struggle to follow even the Ten Commandments. I guess for most of us it's a concoction of religious practices and rituals like observing the Sabbath, eating or not eating certain foods and modes of dress. Individually we adhere to some level or mixture of those things."

"Sounds like most other religions" Bill laughed "Where rituals and dogmas prevail. What about morality though? I mean apart from the Ten Commandments."

"You mean apart from the 613 rules" Ben smiled. "We do have the golden rule, don't forget. The golden rule to love your neighbour as yourself comes from Leviticus 19. The trouble is we find it hard to do. It's hard when Israel is surrounded by neighbours who hate us."

Bill nodded "What about consequences? What do Jews believe are the consequences of obeying Gods laws or not?"

"Of course we believe our actions have consequences. Most of us recognise the concept that you reap what you sow and believe in a hereafter where sins are punished and good deeds are rewarded. Throughout history Jews have believed when our people have been oppressed or enslaved that it was a punishment for our sins."

"That seems to have happened a few times in Jewish history" Bill said rather cheekily.

"Yeah we're big sinners" Ben joked. "We've been through some rough times in our history. Some pretty bad stuff happened right here" Ben waved his hand towards the window as the guide announced they were approaching Masada where 960 Zealots had held off the Romans for three years before finally committing suicide rather than being taken slave.

After a fun swim in the Dead Sea they finally arrived in Jerusalem where they would spend the next several days.

On the first day they visited the Shrine of the Book, a part of the Israel Museum that was purpose built to house the Dead Sea Scrolls. After a brief tour their guide offered them time to themselves. Bill was particularly interested in the adjacent model of Jerusalem based on an understanding of the city as it was prior to its destruction by the Romans in 70 AD. While the rest of the group looked around the museum Bill and Sarah found themselves alone in the courtyard that housed the large spectacular model. Bill was leaning over the model trying to get a good photograph of the temple when he was startled by a voice "Impressive isn't it?"

He turned to see an old gentleman with a long grey beard smiling at him. "Oh yes, it's amazing" Bill replied. "I was just trying to get a better photo of the temple. It must have been magnificent in its day."

The old man nodded "Yes it was beautiful, but the bricks and mortar of the temple itself are not what's important. The earthly temple was merely a symbolic representation of God's Holy Temple in heaven. The temple, its layout, furnishings and even the rituals are allegorical. Together they explain the meaning of our lives and our relationship with God."

"The meaning of our lives" Bill remarked with interest. "How does that work?"

"Well for example there are three main zones in the temple, the Outer Courtyard, the Holy Place and the Holy of Holies. Each of these three areas had its own level of sacredness and special meaning. The Outer Court was the area accessible to the ordinary Israelite, where a person starts their journey towards perfection of their soul through sacrifice and the achievement of knowledge and virtue. The Temple furniture represents virtue and knowledge. The Holy Place was the second level which was only allowed to be accessed by the priests and finally there was the Holy of Holies housing the Ark of the Covenant, symbolising the presence of God. This most sacred sanctuary was only accessed by the High Priest once a year and represents the end of man's journey; the highest level of advancement of the human soul, where man meets God."

"That's fascinating" Bill remarked. "Three levels, three chambers." He looked at Sarah "That sounds familiar."

Sarah nodded back.

The old man looked curiously at Bill and said "My name is Avi by the way."

"Pleased to meet you Avi, my name is Bill and this is my wife Sarah. So how do you know this stuff Avi and where did the design come from?"

"Well the allegorical meaning of it all has been somewhat esoteric but we have some record of the concepts in the writings of Philo of Alexandria. Of course the actual design for the Temple itself was given by God to King David who passed it on to his son Solomon. But it follows the same basic layout with the three zones as the portable Tabernacle that was constructed according to the instructions given to Moses by God on Mount Sinai. The portable Tabernacle was the House of God used on the journey from Mount Sinai to the Promised Land."

"Could the design be more ancient, and say, have come from Egypt?" Billed suggested.

"Well of course that's where the Israelites were coming from. And the design of the Tabernacle and the Ark of the Covenant are similar to Egyptian relics. So I suppose that's possible."

"Tell me more about the symbolism of the Temple" Bill continued. "How is the Temple on Earth connected to the spiritual Temple?"

"The earthly Temple is a mirror reflection of the celestial temple in the spirit world. What we do in the physical world with our physical existence is reflected in the spiritual world, the world of God, on which our souls reside. Our aim is to move our soul from the material to the spiritual world. That is symbolised by the High Priest entering the Holy of Holies. The High Priest in the spirit realm is the intermediary between God and man, sometimes known as the Logos."

"Christ" Sarah suggested.

"Yes that's the Christian perspective" Avi agreed. "Leviticus 16 describes a temple ritual wherein the blood of goats and a bull are offered for the atonement of sins. According to the Epistle to the Hebrews, Christ is the High Priest of the celestial temple and offered His own blood for the redemption of our sins."

"The new covenant" Sarah nodded.

"Yes, that's right" Avi agreed.

Just then a member of their tour group came out and beckoned them. They said goodbye to the mysterious Avi and re-joined the group. As they walked to the bus Bill remarked to Sarah "That was interesting what Avi was saying about the symbolism of the Temple. It reminds me of the Freemasons. Their temples are replicas of Solomon's temple and they conduct various rituals symbolising the progress of a man's soul. I understand that as they progress through the various degrees of knowledge and virtue, ceremonies are conducted involving the passage into the three chambers of Solomon's temple, the objective being to reach the Sanctuary."

The tour continued and they visited various tourist sites in Jerusalem and Bethlehem. Bill thought that the places associated with Biblical events were somewhat speculative, but felt that it didn't really matter because it gave the pilgrims a sense of being in a very special place. The highlight for Bill was in a small cave on the Mount of Olives where tradition holds Christ had taught his disciples to say the Lord's Prayer. As the guide was explaining the significance of the cave, it gave Bill goose bumps when the whole group broke into spontaneous prayer saying:

> *"Our Father, who art in heaven*
> *hallowed be thy Name,*
> *thy kingdom come,*
> *thy will be done,*
> *on earth as it is in heaven.*
> *Give us this day our daily bread*

And forgive us our trespasses,
as we forgive those
who trespass against us.
And lead us not into temptation,
but deliver us from evil.
For thine is the kingdom,
and the power, and the glory,
for ever and ever.
Amen."

On the third day in Jerusalem they visited Mount Moriah, to the Jews the Temple Mount, the site of their once great temple; for Muslims the Dome of the Rock, the place where they believe Muhammad ascended to heaven. As their guide moved them fairly quickly past the mosques where non-Muslims were no longer welcome, Bill said to Sarah "It's a terrible shame what's become of this rock. The site on which a temple was built that symbolised man's love of God and for each other, has instead become a symbol of hatred and intolerance."

Sarah replied "If only they would make the whole site a place of worship available to the people of all three Abrahamic religions to share. That way it could become a symbol of peace and mutual respect and a monument to remind us of the golden rule to love your neighbour as yourself."

Bill shook his head sadly "That's a lovely thought Sarah, but the way things are it can never happen. If anything it's getting worse. Both Muslim's and Jews believe it's their birthright. Children of both sides are taught this hatred too, so that ensures the conflict continues to the next generation. The problem can't be solved because there is no compromise, no tolerance and no forgiveness."

After the busy tourist trails of Jerusalem it was a welcome relief to spend a few days in Northern Israel in the Galilee region. The peace and tranquillity of Galilee was in keeping with the Prince of peace who once lived and taught in this beautiful place. Sailing on the lake from Capernaum to Magdala was the perfect icing on the cake.

On the return journey to Tel Aviv they stopped in Haifa to visit the Bahai temple. Bill and Sarah stood admiring the immaculate gardens. "Isn't this place magnificent?" Sarah said.

"It sure is" Bill agreed "What a wonderful product of man's creativity, love and reverence. Actually when you think about it, all man's great religious buildings and monuments symbolise our creativity, love and devotion to God. And you could extend that idea to include all man's achievements: our industry, exploration, agriculture, engineering . . ."

"Gardens" Sarah offered.

"Yes and isn't this one a fine example of man's use of the resources God gave him to create an object of such beauty and majesty. It's a symbol of the selflessness, devotion, and love that's potentially in each and every one of us" Bill sighed contentedly "God would be proud of His creation I think."

Their final night in Tel Aviv was quite magical. It was a Saturday night and many people were out celebrating. There were street musicians, a huge open air folk dance next to the beach, restaurants were buzzing with sounds of enjoyment and laughter. Bill and Sarah walked out along the causeway to the lighthouse by the boat harbour. Young couples walked past hand in hand, people were fishing from the rocks. The peaceful sound of the lapping water blended with the distant dance music. The peace was suddenly disturbed by the sound of an aircraft flying overhead. Bill looked up "Oh my God is that a drone?" he said.

"Surely not" Sarah replied.

"It looks like a drone" Bill said. A shiver went down his spine. "Aren't you glad we live in Australia?"

"Yes, and I'll be glad to get home" Sarah replied.

The next day they started the journey home. Soon after their return to Australia Bill went to a Junto meeting and was able to spend some time with Hamish.

"So Bill did you find out what is the meaning of life?"

"Yes I think so" Bill responded "The meaning of life is to perfect our souls."

Hamish nodded "And how do we do that?"

"The consensus among sages is that we should seek out the truth for ourselves about what's right and then do it. The main difficulty seems to be figuring out what is the Truth and therefore what's right. When I looked at the major religions I found a lot of dogma but there are a few simple truths that transcend them all I think."

"What are those?"

"That we have a soul which lives on after we die, that we are free to choose our thoughts and to choose right or wrong, that we reap what we sow and above all that we should obey the golden rule to treat others as we would have them treat us."

"Is that it?"

"Yes that's about it."

Hamish stared disapprovingly at Bill "Do you mean to tell me that after all that travelling, research and philosophising that's all you could come up with?"

Bill squirmed uncomfortably "Um pretty much yes" he replied sheepishly.

Hamish roared with laughter "I'm just teasing you Bill; I think you've summed it up nicely."

Bill grinned, sighing with relief. "One thing that still puzzles me though Hamish is whether there really is a secret Brotherhood who watch over us, teaching the Truth and helping us along the way."

Hamish seemed to drift off into thought for a few moments before replying "Bill I'm absolutely sure there is a Brotherhood of Truth but it's no secret. Anyone who upholds and teaches Truth is part of that Brotherhood. We don't need mystery schools to teach us Truth, we have the school of life. Everyone we encounter may be a teacher or a student. The trouble with many people is that when they find the Truth they don't believe it unless they think it comes from some perceived higher authority, whether it's a saint or messenger from God or whatever."

"Yes I've noticed that" Bill agreed. "I find that when I tell someone that this idea or fact came from someone else such as some mysterious higher source they are more inclined to accept it."

"That's right Bill, unfortunately people may not take notice of you when they know you. Even Christ had this problem."

137

"A prophet is not without honour, but in his own country, and among his own kin, and in his own house" Bill suggested quietly.

"Exactly" Hamish concurred. "It's one of the peculiarities of human nature that we are often more concerned with where the idea came from than whether the idea is True or not. This unfortunate fact has been the cause of many cults and religions both good and bad. When someone claims that God or a saint or an angel gave him a particular idea he can create a whole army of followers whereas if he said he thought up the idea himself, then likely no one would take any notice."

"It's a sad state of affairs" Bill muttered "That people take more notice of the messenger than the message itself. So where does that leave me? Will anyone take any notice of the ideas in my books? Have I wasted my time?"

Hamish reached over and patted Bill on the shoulder "Some will yes. They may be few but they are important. Don't be impatient. Some will find the ideas in your books after you have passed from this life. Perhaps you yourself will even find them when you return in a future life. Through your books you have become a teacher.

The right people will find your books. They will be people who are at a particular stage on their journey. You can't help everyone. There are some highly educated people who believe they can solve the world's problems by helping the lowly, or so-called disadvantaged folk. But they end up in heartache and despair because their well-intentioned efforts are futile."

"I think I know what you mean" Bill nodded "I once knew a teacher who was highly educated and he went to teach at a low socioeconomic urban school, thinking that was where he could do the most good. But after many years of battling he realised that he was making little difference. Most of the kids didn't want to learn, classes were a nightmare of disruption and chaos. Eventually he went to teach at a private school where the kids were bright and wanted to learn. He's now happy and enjoys the rewards of helping these advanced students to progress to great heights."

Hamish nodded "And we can do the same Bill, our job is to move both ourselves and those around us who are willing from mediocrity to greatness."

Conclusion

"I with an unbiased indifferency followed Truth, wither I thought she lead me." John Locke

This has been a story like many religious stories of the past, some true, some mythical and some a combination of truth and myth. Stories are good because we remember them and we enjoy them but it is the morals embedded into our stories that really count. Christ told parables to help us understand His message. Plato used his conversations with Socrates to convey his messages. Stories change throughout history to appeal to particular audiences, but the simple Truths remain constant.

I have endeavoured through this story to find the common threads of Truth from some of the great Teachers who have devoted their lives to others and have loved God through their love of mankind. They have taught the simple Truth that we are here to perfect our souls, which requires us to figure out for ourselves what is right and then *do* it. No one can do it for us. We must take responsibility to uplift ourselves. Our Creator gave us free will to choose our thoughts, to choose our actions and the ability to reason what is right and what is wrong. We can be certain that we will reap the benefits of our right actions and suffer the consequences of our wrong actions. Above all, the great Ones have taught us the golden rule to treat others as we would like to be treated.

The meaning of life isn't some great mysterious unsolvable riddle. The great Truths are simple and are available to anyone who cares to look. We don't have to be "intellectuals" to figure it out. In fact, being an intellectual may be a handicap because it often leads to the garbage of relativism and puts political correctness over common sense.

Truth is not about dogmas and rituals, it's about the way we live our lives and how we treat our fellow man. It's about knowledge and virtue. While the Truths are simple, their application and interaction with one another is not so easy. That's why I think our souls have been allotted a number of lifetimes to learn to apply them on a case by case basis. The achievement of this wisdom may be called enlightenment or sainthood.

All of us will likely harbour some false beliefs, including me. We have false beliefs for various reasons: perhaps because we were taught false ideas as a child and have never properly considered them in light of our experiences. Perhaps we were converted to false ideas by a charismatic leader or an authority figure whose confidence in their own false convictions has overpowered us. Perhaps we are too frightened to think because of the threat of being excluded from our comfortable group: our family, our friends or our religion. Perhaps we were blinded into false belief by the passion of being in love. Because of these factors we must continually reflect on our beliefs and test them using our God given powers of reason and our experiences. We should not take anything for granted, especially from those in authority.

I may not have the right answers about the nature of existence, but what I have tried to demonstrate is that religious understanding can be rational. Truth must always be the ultimate goal and I believe it can be derived through rational thinking applied to the evidence of our observations and experiences. If the Truths we live by can't stand up to the test of reason then we condemn ourselves to a life of self-delusion.

Relatively few people contemplate the big questions of life, preferring to abdicate this responsibility to others. This is a sad state of affairs because often those who do are completely blind to the Truth and they carry the vast majority of humanity along on false trails. These blind leaders enjoy their positions of power and authority over others and do not welcome challengers. Therefore, above all, we must ensure freedom of expression and free speech in our societies, so that Truth can always surface.

God has given you the power of rational thinking, the power of reason. Why not use it to find the Truth for yourself. The Truth will set you free.

Tony Hassall